Staff
Development
Programs

Essential
Tools for
Educators

The Program Evaluation Guides for Schools
Richard M. Jaeger, Series Editor

Terry W. Mullins

Staff Development Programs

A Guide to Evaluation

The Program Evaluation Guides for Schools
Series Editor: Richard M. Jaeger

CORWIN PRESS, INC.
A Sage Publications Company
Thousand Oaks, California 91320

For information address:

 Corwin Press, Inc.
A Sage Publications Company
2455 Teller Road
Thousand Oaks, California 91320

SAGE Publications Ltd.
6 Bonhill Street
London EC2A 4PU
United Kingdom

SAGE Publications India Pvt. Ltd.
M-32 Market
Greater Kailash I
New Delhi 110 048 India

Printed in the United States of America

Library of Congress Cataloging-in-Publication Data

Mullins, Terry Wayne.
    Staff development programs: a guide to evaluation / Terry W. Mullins.
        p.   cm. — (The program evaluation guides for schools)
    Includes bibliographical references (pp. 95-96) and index.
    ISBN 0-8039-6045-X (alk. paper)
    1. Teachers—In-service training—United States—Evaluation.
I. Title II. Series: Essential tools for educators.
LB1731.M85   1994
371.1 ′ 46 ′ 0973—dc20   94-21623

The paper in this book meets the specifications for permanence of the American National Standards Institute and the National Association of State Textbook Administrators.

94 95 96 97 98 10 9 8 7 6 5 4 3 2 1

Corwin Press Production Editor: Diane S. Foster

Contents

Series Editor's Preface

Essential Tools for Educators: The Program Evaluation Guides for Schools is a series grounded in the premise that regular evaluation of school programs can be of enormous help to school professionals—provided they are the ones who plan the evaluations, conduct the evaluations, and use the evaluations to guide their school improvement activities. Evaluation is a powerful tool for documenting school needs, identifying strengths and weaknesses in school programs, and discovering how to improve almost every aspect of school life. Program evaluation need not be complex or inordinately time consuming. Simple principles and strategies are described in the initial volume of this series, *Evaluating School Programs: An Educator's Guide*. Then, specific techniques and approaches are illustrated in the program-focused guides that complete the series. Using these principles and techniques, teachers, principals, and other school professionals can plan, conduct, and interpret the findings of powerful evaluations of their curricula; of their instructional programs in mathematics, reading, language arts, and special education; of their programs for "at-risk" students; and of their counseling and personnel development programs. The principles to be learned from this series can be applied even more broadly to the evaluation of school disciplinary programs, student assessment programs, community relations programs, and other programmatic elements that are central to the successful functioning of a school.

Extensive technical training is *not* prerequisite to planning and conducting sound evaluations of school programs. Sound evaluation *does* require a desire to improve one's school, willingness to work collegially, careful attention to detail, and basic knowledge of how school program evaluations should be carried out. The ETE series provides school professionals with the last of these elements—the essential tools they need to plan and conduct effective evaluations of their school programs.

Evaluating School Programs: An Educator's Guide is the foundation volume in this series. It contains a clear, concise exposition of the objectives, principles, and core issues that undergird solid evaluations of school programs. By reading this guide, principals and their colleagues will learn how to (a) determine the feasibility of conducting a school program evaluation, (b) focus a school program evaluation, (c) structure and design a school program evaluation, (d) conduct a school program evaluation, (e) interpret the results of a school program evaluation, (f) report and make use of the results of a school program evaluation, and (g) ensure that a school program evaluation is conducted ethically, damages no one, and enriches all who are associated with the program being evaluated.

Once these basic elements of a school evaluation are well understood, readers will be ready to proceed to the guide in this series that focuses on the subject area of the program to be evaluated. Each program-specific guide provides specific instruction on the evaluation of school programs in a single subject area, and each follows a consistent pattern of organization. Following an introduction that provides an overview and rationale for program evaluation in its subject area, each program-specific guide contains a sequence of vignettes (chapters) that illustrate, in detail, evaluation of a focused aspect of a school program. Collectively, these vignettes illustrate how evaluations of school programs are planned, structured, staffed, conducted, interpreted, and used. The vignettes cover a wide range of practical evaluative issues; illustrate the selection, development, and use of a large number of evaluation strategies and instruments; and show how the results of evaluation can be used to strengthen school programs. Resources at the end of each program-specific guide contain a set of research-based standards and indicators of school program quality, a road map to the use of these standards in evaluating the effectiveness and efficiency of a school program, and an annotated bibliography of selected references on program evaluation in the subject area of the guide.

Evaluations can help school professionals make their school the best it can be and, in the process, substantially increase their own educational effectiveness. In the hands of thoughtful, well-trained school professionals, evaluation can be a transformative catalyst that improves schools and all who work and learn in them. The ETE series will help you become one of those distinctive school professionals who can make school program evaluations work well. Knowing that your investment in this knowledge will pay rich dividends for years to come, I wish you every success.

RICHARD M. JAEGER
University of North Carolina
Greensboro

About the Author

Terry W. Mullins is Professor of Management and Dean of the School of Business Administration at the University of Evansville. Previously, he was Academic Dean at Menlo College and chaired the Department of Management and Marketing at the University of North Carolina at Greensboro. In addition to providing leadership for the business school, he teaches strategic management and organizational behavior. He conducts research on management, strategy, and human resources issues. As a researcher and trainer, he is interested in the bridge between theory and practice in both education and management. His research has appeared in scholarly and professional journals such as the *Journal of Applied Psychology, Personnel Psychology,* the *Journal of Labor Research,* and the *American Business Review, Personnel,* and *Personnel Administrator.* As a staff development trainer, he has conducted programs and workshops for school systems throughout the country on leadership, strategy, management, selection procedures, and performance appraisal. He consults with school systems on the implementation and evaluation of staff development programs and projects. He earned his Ph.D. and M.B.A. in Business Administration from the University of Houston. He has a B.A. in Liberal Arts from Raymond College at the University of the Pacific.

Introduction

The Purpose of This Guide

If you are responsible for evaluating staff development programs, as either an evaluation team leader or a team member, this book was designed for you. As a school principal, a staff development coordinator, a teacher or counselor on an evaluation team, or a staff development trainer, you will find this book useful for improving staff development programs in your school.

This guide is designed for clarity and organized for convenience. Although this guide will not turn you into a program evaluation professional, it will provide you with an easy to follow, step-by-step approach to evaluating staff development programs. If you follow the steps in this guide and study the vignettes used to illustrate sound evaluation practices, you will be able to conduct a systematic, valid evaluation of your staff development program.

How to Use This Guide

This book can serve as a "ready reference" for an entire evaluation team. Because most sections of this book are designed to stand alone, you can make good use of this guide without reading it from cover to cover. At least one person on the team, however, preferably the team leader, should read the entire guide. To make best use of this guide, you also should read *Evaluating School Programs: An Educator's Guide,* written by James R. Sanders. Sanders's book is a more comprehensive guide to program evaluation designed specifically for use with this and other specialized evaluation guides in this series. Throughout this book you will be referred to Sanders's *Guide* for more detailed explanations of various evaluation issues.

The quality of your evaluation can be greatly influenced by following a few simple principles of evaluation. Many common evaluation pitfalls can be avoided easily with some careful planning and basic precautions before the evaluation starts. This guide and Sanders's

Guide to evaluation will acquaint you with key principles and alert you to common problems and pitfalls.

Basic Assumptions and Significant Features of This Guide

Underlying Assumptions

Several assumptions influenced the design of this evaluation guide: (a) A committee of school personnel (teachers, counselors, administrators, etc.) will be responsible for the evaluation; (b) Most committees will not have an evaluation specialist among its members; and (c) Most evaluation teams will carry out their evaluation duties in addition to their regular, full-time responsibilities.

Given these assumptions, this guide presents the basic principles of sound evaluation of staff development programs in straightforward, jargon-free language. Clear and detailed vignettes are used to show how evaluation principles should be applied.

This guide shows you how to select an evaluation team, outlines the responsibilities of the team, specifies the tasks that must be accomplished, and provides advice on implementing the team's recommendations. Special emphasis is given to determining what data or information should be collected and how they should be analyzed and interpreted. Specific advice is offered on designing questionnaires, conducting interviews, and coordinating focus groups. The guide is particularly careful not to shy away from showing you how to deal with the conflict, resistance, and obstructionism that sometimes accompanies the evaluation process.

The vignettes provide rich, realistic examples of evaluation situations. The vignettes are short stories about evaluation problems in schools, with a focus on staff development programs. Attempting to apply abstract concepts in familiar settings, the vignettes are designed to show you how to identify the problems to be evaluated and the steps you need to take to complete the task. At the end of each vignette, there is a summary of the evaluation principles used. There is also advice on alternate approaches to evaluation that also could have been used.

Throughout the vignettes you will be referred to various sections of James Sanders's book, *Evaluating School Programs: An Educator's Guide*. Sanders's book was written to be used as a companion to this volume and was designed to provide you with detailed discussions of evaluation issues. Familiarity with Sanders's work will help you handle difficult evaluation problems with confidence.

Standards and Indicators

The "standards and indicators" approach to evaluation is a significant feature of this series of evaluation guides. For each guide in this series, the research literature related to the evaluation of programs was studied to determine the characteristics of highly effective programs. This survey of the literature resulted in the identification of 10 standards characteristic of effective staff development programs. A *standard* is defined as a characteristic that a program must possess to be consistent with good professional practice, effectiveness, and efficiency in a specified area. Specific measures of those standards were also identified. Measures of a standard were termed *indicators*. An indicator is an outcome, measure, or condition that provides information concerning the extent to which a particular standard is being met. A comprehensive list of standards and indicators of quality is provided in Resource A of this guide.

Why Evaluate?

The evaluation of staff development programs is a time-consuming and somewhat demanding task. Teachers, administrators, and other school personnel are busy people facing full days and crowded agendas every day. Making time for an extra task such as program evaluation is difficult. Yet regular, thorough program evaluations are essential for increasing a school's effectiveness. Program evaluation answers several questions.

1. Are our staff development efforts responsive to the needs of the teachers and the school?
2. Do we have the right staff development programs in place?
3. Should any of our current programs be curtailed or eliminated?
4. Should any of our current programs be expanded?
5. Should we add new programs?
6. How can we continuously improve our programs?

Focus on Program Improvement

The objective of this book is to teach you to evaluate staff development programs in a way that leads to program improvement. This type of evaluation is called formative or developmental evaluation because it examines programs with an eye to enhancing, improving, augmenting, or supplementing their effectiveness. From this perspective, evaluation team members should be seen more as coaches than judges. Staff development programs shaped by appropriate evaluation ensure that developmental needs of teachers and other school personnel are met. A systematic response to professional development needs as well as program needs is one of the most beneficial results of the evaluation process.

Formative evaluation provides an opportunity for people throughout the school and school district to influence staff development activities. Teachers, counselors, and other members of the professional staff can be surveyed or interviewed concerning the appropriateness of topics and effectiveness of staff development trainers. Because programs within each school compete for limited resources, a well-designed and carefully conducted formative evaluation can provide a rationale for obtaining additional resources such as additional personnel, better equipment, more supplies, or curriculum support materials. All programs are likely to need additional resources, but not all programs are equally worthy of additional support. A well-designed evaluation can provide justification for added support.

How to Evaluate a Staff Development Program

Who Should Be on the Evaluation Team?

Team Responsibilities   Evaluation of staff development programs should be conducted by a team. Evaluation team members should be appointed by the principal or school superintendent. Because the results of an evaluation can have a major impact on the school, those appointed to the evaluation team should appreciate the importance of the task. The team should be composed of dedicated, responsible professionals who are knowledgeable about staff development programs and practices—teachers, counselors, and principals make good candidates. The administrator who forms the evaluation team should stress the seriousness of the group's responsibilities. When providing the team with its charge and instructions, the principal (or superintendent) should specify the evaluation task, identify resources available to the team, and establish a deadline for completing the evaluation.

It is necessary to select a person to head the project team. The characteristics of the team leader are extremely important. The team leader should have credibility with teachers, administrators, and other school personnel to obtain the commitment and cooperation needed for the task. Program expertise is also essential.

Leading the Evaluation Team

The Team Leader's Job   The responsibility for coordinating an evaluation is substantial. The task is sometimes complex and time consuming, although it need not always be so. Unless the evaluation team leader has administrative experience, the management of an evaluation may seem daunting. The team leader needs technical, managerial, and interpersonal skills to accomplish the job.

Technical responsibilities include providing leadership for defining the scope of the project, selecting or creating data collection instruments or forms, analyzing the data, and presenting the results.

Depending on the background of the team leader, many of the required skills and responsibilities may be unfamiliar.

There are significant managerial responsibilities in coordinating an evaluation team. The team leader must staff the project, organize the work, coordinate the efforts of team members, make a large number of significant and trivial decisions, and supervise the people on the team. These tasks must be accomplished on time and within budget. Given the team leader's limited authority, cooperation needs to be obtained voluntarily.

The team leader must possess the interpersonal skills to interact effectively with people at different levels of the school organization who carry out a variety of functions. The project leader and other team members must be tactful, politic, and persuasive. The skills of motivating, coaching, and cajoling people may well come into play before the team completes its work.

Evaluation efforts must gain support throughout the school. Otherwise, resistance to change can stymie needed improvements. Gaining such support is primarily, but not solely, the responsibility of the team leader. First, support for the evaluation efforts must exist among the school's administration. If the evaluation occurs at the school level, the principal's endorsement is essential. At a minimum, the principal should send a memorandum to stakeholders explaining the team's purpose and responsibilities. In addition, the principal should endorse the evaluation in a public meeting. If the team is responsible for a district-wide evaluation, the superintendent should endorse the project publicly.

Support for the evaluation process also must be developed throughout the school or district. Inviting stakeholders to participate in structuring the evaluation process should foster commitment throughout the school or district. Initial support can be maintained by keeping people well informed about the project's progress.

Organizing for Effectiveness

As its first task, the evaluation team needs to organize its work, dividing the project into activities, which in turn are divided into small, manageable tasks. To prevent tasks from falling between the cracks, every aspect of the project must be someone's specific responsibility. Because most tasks cannot be accomplished immediately, milestones marking the project's progress should be created.

Establish target dates for each milestone, and devise a realistic schedule that makes allowances for likely problems and uncertainties. If the committee estimates that 3 days are required to conduct interviews with teachers, the schedule should include an extra day for unforeseen problems.

If your evaluation project is large enough, it may require a budget. The evaluation team may need to purchase tests, questionnaires, or other evaluation forms from publishers. You may need a budget for extra clerical assistance, materials, or the fees for a consultant to analyze and interpret the data. In addition to funds, other resources may need to be budgeted as well. The evaluation team may need access to clerical support from the school or the district. The team may also need access to the school district's computers or to the expertise of district personnel. Once a budget has been established, the team leader should monitor expenses closely.

Once the final evaluation report is complete, the evaluation team should work with the principal, staff development coordinator, or superintendent to create a plan for implementing any recommended changes. As in other stages of the evaluation, the involvement of major stakeholders in developing a schedule for implementing proposed changes is essential.

Focusing the Evaluation

Because it is not possible to evaluate every aspect of every program, your evaluation will need a focus. When developing an evaluation plan, it is necessary to choose what to evaluate. What is to be evaluated is guided by *why* the evaluation is being done, and *how* the results are going to be used.

Use Systematic Procedures

An effective evaluation uses systematic procedures that can stand up to scrutiny and debate. A formative evaluation must be able to withstand rigorous examination, because decisions affecting teachers, students, and budgets are based on the results of the evaluation. During the first stage of evaluation it is important to establish the purposes of the evaluation. Identifying the purposes of the evaluation makes it possible to formulate the questions that will have to be answered as part of the evaluation. The evaluation team should begin to formulate these questions by talking with as many of the stakeholders of the staff development program as possible.

The relevant stakeholders would usually include teachers, program coordinators, school principals, staff development trainers, and those who design the staff development curriculum and materials. An important source of evaluation questions is the standards and indicators in Resource A of this book. These standards and indicators are based on research literature related to good professional practice for staff development programs. It would also be appropriate, although very time consuming and costly, to look at exemplary staff development programs throughout the country and to compare the characteristics of those programs to your own.

External Standards of Quality

In addition to considering the needs of immediate stakeholders, the evaluation team may need to compare the school's staff development program to external standards of quality, such as the Standards and Indicators of Quality included in Resource A of this guide. Also relevant may be guidelines for staff development set by national professional organizations, standards implicit in recognized model programs of staff development, and standards derived from the professional research literature on staff development.

At this point you will have collected a large number of potential evaluation questions. This list of questions is likely to be far too long for every question to be included in an evaluation. Consequently, the next step is to reduce the questions to a manageable number. Use the following criteria to eliminate unnecessary questions:

1. How important is the question, given the purposes of this evaluation?
2. Are there sources of data for this question?
3. How difficult is it to collect data to answer this question?
4. Are the data available for this question likely to be reliable and valid?
5. Can the data available be analyzed and interpreted in a meaningful manner?

Information related to particular evaluation questions can be collected using a variety of forms, scales, and instruments. Potential measurement tools include tests, surveys, questionnaires, interviews, attitude scales, checklists, and systematic observation. Data also can be collected by examining files, records, and archives and by tabulating pertinent information.

Data Collection Issues

Once the committee decides on appropriate evaluation questions, data collection forms or instruments need to be selected or developed. Evaluation questions can seldom be answered directly. Some sort of measuring device, which may range from a standardized instrument to simply observing program activities, must be used. A listing of possible data sources related to the evaluation questions is a good starting point. Frequently, the information needed to evaluate a program can be provided by the people we have identified as stakeholders—teachers, staff development trainers, principals, assistant principals, counselors, program directors, students, and, perhaps, parents. If you collect information from these sources you will probably use interviews, questionnaires, attitude scales, checklists, or focus groups.

Information also can be collected from files or other physical records. The school district's staff development coordinator may have extensive records on staff development programs conducted throughout the year. If so, these records constitute rich data sources. Records may include portfolios of materials, participants' evaluation forms, and the assessments of staff development activities conducted by staff development trainers or coordinators. Examining records systematically requires carefully prepared data collection instruments. In all likelihood, the evaluation team will have to develop its own forms for retrieving information from files and records.

Direct observation, guided by an observation form, is a third approach to gathering evaluative information. Systematic observation is difficult and requires more skill and training than other methods discussed. If systematic observation is the best way to evaluate your program, it may be appropriate to hire a consultant experienced in studying the behavior that should be observed.

Use Multiple Sources of Information

Where possible, a given research question should be explored using more than one source of information. If it is possible to obtain information from multiple sources, the results will be more reliable and more accurate. Just as a journalist verifies information for a newspaper story by talking to more than one person, cross-checking your data will improve the accuracy of your findings. Having identified the possible data sources for a given evaluation question, the team must select a suitable data collection device. The advantages and disadvantages of each of several data collection devices are explored briefly below.

A test is one of the most commonly used mechanisms for collecting data. Classroom teachers have considerable experience in devising and using tests. A test provides the advantage of collecting a large amount of information quickly and cheaply under standardized circumstances. There are two types of tests: standardized tests and custom-designed (homemade) tests. Standardized tests have been carefully designed and may have established norms and come with extensive information on reliability and validity. When an appropriate standardized test is available to assess your particular evaluation question, you should consider its use carefully. A standardized test not only saves time and effort, it can also provide reliable and valid information when used appropriately.

If a standardized test is not available, it is possible to devise a test for the activity you are assessing. By developing your own test, your team can pinpoint the issues important to your program. The primary disadvantages of homemade tests are lack of norms and little information about the test's reliability or validity.

Opinions about staff development issues can be collected with questionnaires and surveys containing attitude scales. Questionnaires and surveys share many of the advantages enjoyed by tests. Questionnaires and surveys can be quickly and inexpensively administered to a large number of people, and they lend themselves to standardized administration procedures, reducing the chances of collecting unreliable data.

As is the case with tests, standardized questionnaires exist to measure a number of important concepts and attitudes. If standardized attitude measurements or opinion surveys matching your evaluation questions are available and appropriate to your purposes, use them in preference to developing your own.

If you develop your own questionnaire, write your questions using simple, straightforward language that communicates clearly to your respondents. The questions should be written for clarity and ease of reading. Be certain to avoid "double-barreled" questions, which ask two questions in one.

Complex, ambiguous, and poorly understood issues cannot be addressed effectively with tests or survey instruments. In this situation, an interview is frequently the most effective tool. In an interview, issues can be explored at length and in detail. The interviewer can probe an initial response to discover the respondent's exact meaning in a way not possible with a questionnaire or a test. This advantage is counterbalanced by the level of skill and the amount of time required to conduct an interview effectively. Interviewers must be trained thoroughly and carefully to avoid bias and lack of objectivity.

Checklists devised specifically for your staff development program can provide you with a wealth of information concerning program practices and procedures. For many of the standards and indicators identified in Resource A, a checklist can serve as a major data collection tool. Checklists are particularly appropriate when an evaluation question can be answered with a "yes" or "no" item (or a series of "yes" and "no" items). One of the major advantages of a checklist is the simplicity of the associated data collection procedure. Because the level of subjective judgment needed to use a checklist is low, raters require relatively little training. The primary disadvantage of a checklist is that the evaluation team must develop its own forms because there are relatively few standardized checklists.

Systematic observation can be used to obtain information about how staff development activities are implemented. For example, systematic observation would be an effective way to assess the use of adult learning theory principles by staff development trainers. Systematic observation can also be used to measure the extent to which concepts and skills taught in staff development programs have been implemented.

Systematic observation has two major advantages. First, the evaluator has the opportunity for first-hand observation of the variables of interest. Second, the technique can be applied in a variety of situations, and the data collected is extremely rich. The same cautions apply to systematic observation as applied to both interviews and the development of custom measurement devices. Unless carefully trained, observers can introduce bias and unreliability into the data. This can be a particular problem when an observer has a vested interest in the positive evaluation of a program. The best way to reduce these threats is to develop comprehensive observation protocols and train the observers to use them objectively.

Match Data Collection to Evaluation Questions   Before finalizing data collection strategies and forms, the committee should compare each instrument to corresponding evaluation questions. This procedure will ensure that the data generated are responsive to the evaluation questions. The following questions can help you assess the appropriateness of data collection strategies and forms:

1. Is there at least one data collection device for each evaluation question?
2. Are there multiple measures or data collection strategies for the more complex and ambiguous questions to be answered?
3. Does the data collection form or instrument target data directly pertinent to answering the evaluation question?
4. Does the data collection form or instrument provide all the data needed to answer the evaluation questions comprehensively and unambiguously?
5. If you cannot obtain access to your preferred data source, are there additional data sources and/or alternative data collection strategies available?

Data Collection Strategies

Your approach to collecting information should be complex enough to accomplish the job, but no more so. Your data collection strategy should be guided by the type of data to be collected, the sources of data, the time available, and other resources at your disposal.

Census or Sample   In addition to selecting instruments, the committee will have to decide how much data to collect. Should a census be taken or will a sample suffice? When data are collected from all potential subjects or when all records are examined, a census of the population has been conducted. A census is more accurate than a sample because it provides a complete and comprehensive examination of the data. Consequently, a census is preferred over a sample when it is feasible. A census is not practical or necessary for extremely large populations, however. Careful sampling procedures produce a highly accurate picture of the total population.

The evaluation team should strive to select a sample that is representative of the population from which it is drawn. If respondents are selected randomly (every nth person, for example), the sample should be representative. Determining the appropriate sample size is a complex technical problem, but one rule of thumb is that little confidence can be placed in very small samples. Most statistics based on samples smaller than 100 are not very reliable unless, of course, the population is also very small.

In general, samples of convenience should be avoided. A sample of convenience is any subset of the population that is surveyed simply because it is easy to obtain responses. Convenience samples are undesirable because they are frequently unrepresentative of the population.

Training of Data Collectors

Some simple training for your team will improve your chances of collecting information that is complete, unbiased, and accurate. At a minimum, team members need to be cautioned and trained to avoid clerical errors. Using standardized instructions when administering a test, survey, or questionnaire improves the reliability of results. In more subjective, face-to-face data collection situations, evaluators should use standardized interview protocols, checklists, or behavior observation scales. The forms used to tabulate the data should have a simple design that promotes clerical accuracy.

Reliability and Validity   Valid conclusions can only be drawn from reliable information. A reliable measure is one that produces consistent results when the same variable is measured repeatedly for the same person or program over a short time period. Data collectors should be trained to evaluate complex data sources (answers to interview questions, for example) in a consistent manner. Consistency among data collectors enhances the reliability of the data and ultimately increases the confidence that can be placed in the conclusions drawn from the data.

Data collected by evaluation team members should be free of personal bias. Members of the evaluation team will have their own opinions, values, and agendas regarding the staff development program under evaluation. It is important, however, that their personal values and interests do not influence their data collecting. To put it bluntly, evaluation team members must not fudge the data. Furthermore, there are more subtle and complex issues involved as well. When a team member conducts an interview, for example, the questions should be asked in a professional manner that does not suggest the answer the interviewer would prefer to hear. Interviewers should be trained to collect data using a formal interview protocol. An interview protocol is the set of written questions arranged in a predetermined order to be asked of each interviewee. Role-playing is a particularly effective technique for training interviewers to conduct professional, unbiased, reliable, and accurate interviews.

Organizing and Analyzing Data

Data should be collected systematically, stored securely, and accessed only by those with a legitimate professional or administrative need for the data. Backup copies of unprocessed data need to be maintained to ensure against mishaps. Members of the evaluation team should be cautioned to treat all data collected as confidential.

Planning the Data Analysis

The type of data analysis required depends on a number of factors. In planning your data analysis, your committee should first determine how complex an analysis is required. A highly sophisticated data analysis is not always necessary. If only minor program changes are contemplated, a very simple presentation of data may suffice. If a comprehensive evaluation of a program is appropriate, more sophisticated data analysis procedures may be required. The committee will need to decide early in the project how the data analysis will be conducted.

On some evaluation teams, one or more members will be capable of doing the needed data analysis. Other teams may not be so fortunate. If you do not have a skilled data analyst on your committee, it may be advisable to seek the help of a statistical consultant, such as a person from your school system's central office evaluation staff. If an outside statistical consultant is to be used, involve that person in the earliest stages of the evaluation design process. An outside evaluation consultant can provide the committee with invaluable assistance in identifying data to be collected, in selecting the data collection instruments, and in the analysis and interpretation of the data itself. The early involvement of a statistical consultant will both simplify and accelerate the data analysis.

In situations where standardized instruments can be used, the data analysis procedures are relatively straightforward. Standardized tests, attitude scales, and observational checklists should have established norms and estimates of their reliabilities and validities. The norms provided will usually include means and standard deviations for specific items and for the instrument as a whole. When norms are available, it is possible to make a direct comparison between the results obtained for your school and results obtained in other schools. Makers of standardized tests may also provide you with information that helps you interpret your own scores.

Unfortunately, standardized instruments will not be available for many of your data collection purposes. Your committee may find it necessary to develop its own tests, surveys, questionnaires, attitude scales, and checklists. These instruments are quite valuable because they will allow you to pinpoint particular characteristics and needs of your program. Interpretation of data will, however, be more difficult and less certain because the results cannot be compared to established standards or norms. This means that great care must be used in interpreting the results from homemade instruments devised for your evaluation.

Involving Stakeholders

The results of your findings will have different meanings for different groups of people, and the implications of your findings will vary from group to group. Teachers and administrators may draw very different conclusions from the same data, and the staff development coordinator might reach yet another conclusion. A full discussion of the data and their analysis by all interested parties will improve the quality of the conclusions reached. Participation of stakeholders early in the process increases the likelihood that the results of the report will be accepted and implemented. The involvement of other people from the school and school district will increase the comprehensiveness and complexity of the issues considered by your evaluation team.

One of the best ways to involve stakeholders is to schedule an open meeting for discussion of the implications of the evaluation committee's findings. Approximately 2 weeks prior to the meeting, send each participant a detailed report of the data analyzed by the evaluation team. Each person should be asked to come to the meeting prepared to respond to the following two questions:

1. What are the implications of the results associated with each evaluation question?
2. What changes in programs, if any, would you suggest based on the results presented for each evaluation question?

Providing participants with an opportunity to study the data prior to the meeting will improve the quality of the discussion at the meeting. The meeting provides an opportunity to identify areas of agreement and disagreement within and across stakeholder groups. After areas of basic agreement have been identified, areas of disagreement can be explored in some detail. Not all points of conflict are likely to be resolved in this meeting, but the committee will have a thorough understanding of the views of their stakeholder groups. If controversial issues are involved, the stakeholder meeting should be recorded and transcribed, with the transcription becoming part of the official record of the evaluation. The evaluation team can study the transcript for suggestions that can be incorporated in its final report.

Reporting the Results of the Evaluation Study

In preparing a formal report (assuming one is needed), the evaluation team should consider carefully the needs and interests of the various audiences it must address. The school's administrative team might be a major audience for the study, and this group would likely be interested primarily in a program's effectiveness compared to the resources devoted to it. Almost certainly, the managerial and financial issues facing the superintendent and other administrators will dominate their responses to the evaluation report. Consequently, the evaluation team needs to take these issues into account in preparing its recommendations. Teachers and other professional staff who participate in staff development activities are also important audiences for an evaluation report. Teachers are likely to be concerned with the usefulness of the staff development activities in addressing immediate classroom problems. Teachers likely will be much less concerned with program costs or, perhaps, with broader issues affecting the school district as a whole. Other stakeholders will bring their own priorities to their reading of the report.

To increase its responsiveness to various stakeholder groups, the evaluation committee should circulate a copy of its preliminary report to members of all stakeholder groups. The report should be clearly marked as a draft, and a covering memo should ask for comments and suggestions aimed at improving the final report. The committee should allow itself enough time to consider and weigh the comments and suggestions prior to preparing the final revision of its report. A sample report outline is shown in Table I.1.

Although the committee should not feel bound to follow this report outline, it does offer a good starting place for structuring a team's report. The evaluation team's work is not complete when the final report is submitted. The evaluation team's final responsibility is to work with teachers, administrators, and other stakeholders to implement the report's recommendations.

TABLE I.1. Sample Report Outline

I. Executive Summary

II. Introduction to the Report
    A. Purposes of the evaluation
    B. Audiences for the evaluation report
    C. Limitations of the evaluation and explanation of disclaimers (if any)
    D. Overview of report contents

III. Focus of the Evaluation
    A. Description of the evaluation objectives
    B. Evaluative questions or objectives used to focus the study
    C. Information needed to complete the evaluation

IV. Evaluation Plan and Procedures
    A. Information collection plan; design of the study
    B. Overview of evaluation instruments
    C. Overview of data analysis and interpretation

V. Presentation of Evaluation Results
    A. Summary of evaluation findings
    B. Interpretation of evaluation findings

VI. Conclusions and Recommendations
    A. Criteria and standards used to judge the staff development program
    B. Judgments about the staff development program
    C. Recommendations

VII. Minority Reports or Rejoinders (if any)

VIII. Appendices
    A. Detailed tabulations or analyses of data
    B. Instruments and/or detailed procedures used
    C. Other information

Vignettes and How They Are Organized

Principles and procedures for evaluating staff development programs are difficult to grasp in the abstract. For most people, principles are easier to understand when they are applied to specific problems. The vignettes presented in the next part of this book portray evaluation situations in some detail. The people in the vignettes face complex problems and thorny issues. Frequently, they find that the principles of evaluation they are trying to use do not always fit their situation, and they are not always able to solve all of the problems they face. They are, however, able to use evaluation principles and procedures to conduct their work in a systematic fashion and to learn about the strengths and weaknesses of their staff development programs.

The Vignette Approach

The vignettes should not be regarded as cookbook recipes for you to follow in doing your own evaluation. They are designed to illustrate general strategies for solving some of the more common problems you may face when you evaluate your staff development programs. The vignettes are quite useful in showing you how to prepare for an interview, design a questionnaire, or lay out a data analysis form. They are particularly helpful in showing you how to go from the abstractions represented by the standards and indicators in Resource A to taking the practical steps that will lead to a successful evaluation. Read the vignettes carefully, and think about how you can adapt their solutions to your own evaluation problems.

1

Vignette One

Evaluating Needs Assessment Activities

Background Out the window she could see a middle-aged woman raking leaves in the yard across the street from the playground. The woman, wearing a plaid shirt and jeans, had already amassed two knee-high piles and was working on a third one. The cold frosted her breath. The clear blue sky was punctuated by streaks of gray chimney smoke drifting to the northeast. Two boys, both about 12, tossed a football just outside the window, one pretending to be a quarterback, the other running deep and darting to his left for the catch.

"Damn, another wasted day," muttered Linda Novelli, a second-grade teacher at Jackson Elementary School.

"What's that?" asked Phil Klein, a high school English teacher also looking out the window during the afternoon break in the "Overcoming Math Phobia" workshop.

"Just look at that day out there. An absolutely perfect October day, and we're stuck in here. I wouldn't mind giving up a Saturday if I learned something that would help me teach second grade, but this is a complete waste."

"I guess all those examples of kids overcoming their fears of algebra and geometry are about as useless to you as they are to me."

"Where DO they get the ideas for these workshops?"

Monday morning, Novelli still had that question running around in her head when she passed Ms. Jacobs, her principal, in the hall on the way to her classroom.

"How was the workshop?" asked Ms. Jacobs, a slender African American woman of about 50.

"Funny you should ask. I've been stewing about it all weekend."

"What do you mean?"

"Well, the workshop was on math phobia, and I guess second graders have math phobia, but the trainer didn't talk about problems in the lower grades at all. It was all aimed at middle school and high school kids."

"That's a shame."

"It was even worse for some of the other teachers. Teachers from all grades and all subjects had to suffer through that workshop—art teachers, music teachers, teachers of social studies, English, and history. At least I do teach arithmetic, but those teachers never teach math. How in the world do they decide what topics to cover and who should attend those staff development workshops? That's what I would like to know."

"Well, Linda, I think you have a good point," said Ms. Jacobs, "and I think I'll put that issue on the agenda for the next meeting the principals have with the superintendent."

About 2 weeks later, Linda Novelli found a note from Ms. Jacobs in her office mailbox asking her to stop by the office for a few minutes after classes. About 10 minutes after classes were dismissed, Ms. Novelli entered Ms. Jacobs office.

"Thanks for stopping by. Have a seat," said Ms. Jacobs.

"What's the matter? I've been wondering about your note all day."

"Oh, nothing to worry about. I just wanted to let you know what happened when we discussed the staff development issue at the principals' meeting."

"You really did put it on the agenda?"

"Of course, and I'm glad I did. It seems you're not the only one concerned about staff development issues. Most of the other principals had heard complaints from their teachers, too."

"Well, I'm glad I'm not the only one upset. Are they going to do anything about it?" asked Linda.

"The question is, Are *you* going to do anything about it?"

"What do you mean?"

"Superintendent Skidmore wants you to chair an evaluation team to assess our staff development priorities—if you're willing."

"Why me?"

"Because you obviously care about the issue. You also have a good reputation for getting things done. If you agree to chair the committee, Ms. Skidmore would like to meet with you before you form your committee."

The Evaluation Situation   Linda Novelli met with Superintendent Jean Skidmore on November 15. They discussed the size and composition of the evaluation team, agreeing that the committee should have no more than five members. They also agreed that the committee should have no more than one teacher from each school, no more than one administrator, and that various grade levels and subject areas should be represented.

Within a week, Novelli had her team. The team was composed of Sue Welsch, a middle school principal, Phil Klein, the high school English teacher from the math phobia workshop, Jane Chandler, a middle school science teacher, and Steve Green, a high school marketing education teacher and a member of the district's Staff Development Advisory Committee.

First Team Meeting

Focusing the Evaluation   At the first meeting of the team, Novelli began the meeting with a description of the frustration she and Mr. Klein had felt at the math phobia workshop. Some other members of the team told similar stories, complaining that most of the staff development activities did not address the real needs of teachers. Instead, most of the staff development programs were based on fads, hot topics, and quick fixes. Steve Green protested that these criticisms were unfair. The Staff Development Advisory Committee was very concerned about having good staff development programs, he said.

After some discussion, the group agreed that their objective was to evaluate the methods by which staff development priorities were set, how staff development activities were selected, and how well these matched the needs of the teachers. Novelli reported that although the committee did not have a budget, the superintendent's office would take care of typing, copying, and other clerical support.

"How soon do we have to finish this work?" asked Jane Chandler.

"Ms. Skidmore asked us to be finished by the end of the school year, but I think we should move more quickly than that so we can have some influence on next year's programs."

"The Staff Development Advisory Committee does most of its work in March and April. So if we're done by the end of February, that should work," said Steve Green.

"Is that okay with everyone?" asked Novelli.

Everyone nodded their agreement.

"By the way, why isn't the Staff Development Coordinator on this committee?" asked Green. "After all, Mr. Swensen knows all about the program. Besides, I feel a little bit like a spy, checking up on his programs."

"I'm sure we will talk with Mr. Swensen extensively as we work through this evaluation. I just thought we could be a little more blunt and open about problems if Mr. Swensen was not on the committee."

"You're probably right, but it still makes me uncomfortable," replied Green.

"If it gets to be a major problem, we'll consider putting Mr. Swensen on the committee."

Using Standards and Indicators of Quality

The committee then turned its attention to deciding what needed to be evaluated and how they might go about their task. The standards and indicators in Resource A of this guide provided them with information useful for focusing the evaluation. Standard 2 and Standard 10 were particularly useful:

Standard 2: *Needs Assessment Policy and Procedures.* The school district should have guidelines and procedures for conducting a needs assessment for school-based staff development.

Standard 10: *Participant Contribution.* The school should have formal procedures to allow participants to provide input into the design, evaluation, and modification of the school's staff development program.

Each standard had several indicators that were useful for measuring various aspects of the standard. The evaluation committee compared the standards and indicators to the objective they had set for themselves. After some discussion, they concluded that an evaluation in terms of Standards 2 and 10 would give the team a reasonable basis for recommending needed changes.

"The standards and indicators seem awfully abstract," said Jane Chandler.

"I know what you mean," replied Sue Welsch. "Let's see if we can turn some of this into plain English."

"Well, what are the problems we want to solve or the questions we want to answer?" asked Klein.

"Perhaps 'questions to answer' is the way to think about this," said Novelli. "Let's make a list of questions. Who wants to start?"

They made a list of 16 questions, and then decided they did not have the time or resources to answer that many questions. They finally reduced the questions to 3:

1. Is there a systematic plan for the staff development activities conducted each year?
2. Are the staff development coordinator and the Staff Development Advisory Committee using needs assessment procedures to determine which programs to offer?

3. Do teachers have systematic input into the staff development programs offered?

"This seems to be a manageable list of questions," said Novelli. "Now we just need to figure out how to answer them." After narrowing and focusing the evaluation task, team members were less anxious about completing the job assigned in a timely and effective way.

Data Collection and Analysis

"The first question is easy," said Mr. Green. "Our Staff Development Advisory Committee approves a staff development plan every year. It's required by the State Department of Education to get funding for some of the programs we offer."
"Can you get us a copy of the plan?"
"Sure, no problem."

Identifying Data Sources

After some discussion, the team agreed that they would need several sources of information to answer the second question. First, they decided that they needed to interview members of the Staff Development Advisory Committee as a group. Second, they wanted to interview Mr. Swensen individually. Third, they decided that they needed to see any records that might tell them whether or not needs assessments had been conducted prior to scheduling staff development activities. Linda Novelli agreed to contact the superintendent's office for any records related to needs assessment.

The third question, whether or not teachers had systematic input into the design of programs, generated considerable discussion. Klein and Green had difficulty agreeing.

Dealing With Conflict

"Many of the staff development programs I have attended over the years are good programs—well organized, good handouts, nice audiovisuals, good instructor—but they just don't relate to me," said Klein. "I teach English; that's all I teach. Why did I have to go to a math phobia workshop? There are countless other examples of teachers in this district being required to attend workshops that are not relevant. These may be 'good' programs, but they just do not speak to the needs of the participants."
"I think that's unfair," replied Steve Green. "We work very hard to find programs that will benefit everyone."
"I still think it's stupid for an English teacher to be required to attend math workshops. It's just as stupid when math teachers have to attend writing workshops or 1st-grade teachers have to attend workshops on things that apply only to high school teachers."

TABLE 1.1 Tasks and Responsibilities

Task	Responsibility
1. Get 5 copies of this year's staff development plan	Green
2. Devise a list of questions for interviews with the Staff Development Advisory Committee and Mr. Swensen	Welsch, Klein
3. Obtain records on any needs assessments conducted for staff development programs for the past 3 years	Novelli
4. Devise a checklist for tallying the needs assessment data obtained in Item 3	Green, Chandler
5. Devise a questionnaire for program participants	Novelli, Chandler

"I don't think you appreciate how hard Mr. Swensen and the Staff Development Advisory Committee work to find good programs and good trainers."

"Wait a minute," interrupted Linda Novelli. "Let's not get off on the wrong foot here. I'm sure Mr. Swensen and the members of the Staff Development Advisory Committee all work very hard and are committed to doing a good job. Our job is not to attack Mr. Swensen or the Staff Development Advisory Committee or anyone else. Our job is to evaluate how well the programs presented match the needs of teachers."

"Steve, I know we've put you on the defensive," continued Linda. "I'm sorry. That wasn't our intention. The job of this committee is not to condemn the Staff Development Advisory Committee or Mr. Swensen. Our job is to study the staff development process and see if it can be improved."

"I know I shouldn't be so touchy, but I've worked hard on the Staff Development Advisory Committee, and it's hard to listen to criticism. I promise to keep an open mind."

"Good, that's all I ask."

"Now, let's see if we can get back on track. How can we evaluate the third question? Do teachers have systematic input into the staff development programs offered?"

"How about a survey of teachers who have attended various workshops over the past year or so?" asked Sue Welsch.

TABLE 1.2 Needs Assessment Tally Sheets

Staff Development Activities Offered 1993-1994

	Number	Percentage
Needs assessment completed		
Needs assessment not completed		
Total number of programs		

Staff Development Activities Offered 1992-1993

	Number	Percentage
Needs assessment completed		
Needs assessment not completed		
Total number of programs		

Staff Development Activities Offered 1991-1992

	Number	Percentage
Needs assessment completed		
Needs assessment not completed		
Total number of programs		

"That might work," said Novelli. "What does everyone else think?"

After agreeing to use a survey to collect information about the third question, the team made a list of the things they needed to accomplish before their next meeting. The next meeting was set for Friday of the following week. Each person promised to complete their assigned tasks for the next meeting (see Table 1.1).

Managing the Process
The next day, Steve Green made five copies of the current staff development plan and sent them to the other members of the team through interoffice mail. Anticipating questions about previous staff development plans, Steve also located copies of the staff development plans for the past 3 years.

The following Monday, Steve Green and Jane Chandler met to devise a checklist for tallying the use of needs assessments in justifying staff development activities. Using the staff development plans from the past 3 years, they listed every staff development activity offered in the district. This column was titled Staff Development Activities. In another column, titled Needs Assessment, the words *yes* and *no* appear adjacent to each listed activity. Jane and Steve completed the rough draft of the checklist in about 35 minutes (see Table 1.2).

That same Monday, Linda Novelli made a trip to the superintendent's office immediately after school. The secretary in the superintendent's office was unable to find any files related to needs assessments for staff development activities. Novelli's next stop was Mr. Swensen's office.

TABLE 1.3 Interview Questions: Staff Development Advisory Committee

1. How were each of you selected for this committee?
2. How often does the committee meet?
3. Describe a typical committee meeting.
4. What information about staff development needs comes from teachers and principals?
5. How are priorities for staff development set?
6. Where do ideas for specific programs come from and how are trainers selected?
7. How much input do you have into the annual staff development plan.
8. How are teachers selected for participation in particular staff development activities?
9. How well do you think this committee functions?
10. What would you most like to see changed about this committee?

As she entered the office, Mr. Swensen smiled and said, "I was wondering when I would be getting a visit from you. I hear you are heading a team evaluating staff development activities."

"Well, yes, and I was hoping you could help us."

"Anything you need, just let me know."

"Thanks, there are two things. First, could someone from our group interview you about how the district's staff development priorities are determined and how programs are selected?"

"Sure, anytime. What's thing two?" asked Swensen.

"One of the things the committee has discussed is needs assessment. I was in the superintendent's office asking about records concerning needs assessment and they didn't have anything. I thought maybe you kept those records," said Novelli.

"Sure thing. What records we have on that should be here in my files," replied Swensen. "Let me poke around a little bit here in the files. You want just this year's?" he asked.

"If you have them, it might be helpful to have the past three year's."

Raising his eyebrows, Swensen smiled and said, "That may take some real digging. As you can see from my office, I haven't won any neatness awards lately. Let me give you a call in a day or two when I've turned up those files."

"Okay," said Linda. "We have a committee meeting on Friday and I would like to have the files for that meeting."

"Sure thing."

Preparing for an Interview

Tuesday afternoon, Sue Welsch and Phil Klein met in Welsch's office to work on the interview questions. Based on what she had read in Sanders's *Guide,* Welsch knew that they needed to have a prepared

TABLE 1.4 Interview Questions: Mr. Swensen, Staff Development Coordinator

1. What's the role of the Staff Development Advisory Committee?
2. How often does the committee meet?
3. Describe a typical committee meeting.
4. What information about staff development needs comes from teachers and principals?
5. How are priorities for staff development set?
6. Where do ideas for specific programs come from and how are trainers selected?
7. How great a role does needs assessment play in devising your annual staff development plan?
8. What input do you seek from teachers, principals, and the Staff Development Advisory Committee when preparing the annual staff development plan?
9. How are teachers selected for participation in particular staff development activities?
10. How well do you think your Staff Development Advisory Committee functions?
11. What would you most like to see changed about this committee?

list of questions to conduct their interviews. The list of questions is called the *interview protocol*. The interview protocol helps organize the interview and ensures that no questions are forgotten. When it is important to ask questions in a particular order, an interview protocol provides that structure.

Working to keep the length of their interview with the Staff Development Advisory Committee manageable, Klein and Welsch pared down their initial list of 19 questions to 10. A similar interview protocol was developed for interviewing Mr. Swensen, the Staff Development Coordinator. To make comparisons easier, Welsch and Klein attempted to use the same questions for both Mr. Swensen and the Staff Development Advisory Committee (see Tables 1.3 and 1.4).

Later in the week, Novelli and Chandler met to work on the questionnaire for program participants. After some discussion, they decided to ask two types of questions. The first type of question asked about program quality, and the second type of question asked about how well the program met the needs of respondents. They revised the questions several times before they were satisfied with their questionnaire (see Table 1.5).

The evaluation team met at the end of the week in the conference room at Linda Novelli's school. When everyone had arrived, Steve Green distributed a copy of the current staff development plan to each person. He also told them that he had brought one copy of the staff development plans for the past 3 years. Novelli suggested that each

TABLE 1.5 Staff Development Workshop Questionnaire

Program Name _____

INSTRUCTIONS: Please respond to the following statements concerning the program listed above. There are no right or wrong responses to the statements listed below. Circle the response that most closely describes your opinion concerning the item. Do not put your name on this form. All responses are anonymous and confidential.

Program Quality

1. The content of this program was logically organized and presented.

   Strongly Agree   Agree   Neutral   Disagree   Strongly Disagree

2. The trainer was well prepared.

   Strongly Agree   Agree   Neutral   Disagree   Strongly Disagree

3. The support materials (handouts, overheads, slides, exercises, etc.) were effective.

   Strongly Agree   Agree   Neutral   Disagree   Strongly Disagree

Program Relevance

4. I learned things in this workshop that I can apply in my classroom.

   Strongly Agree   Agree   Neutral   Disagree   Strongly Disagree

5. This program was relevant to problems I face as a teacher.

   Strongly Agree   Agree   Neutral   Disagree   Strongly Disagree

6. I am a better teacher because of this workshop.

   Strongly Agree   Agree   Neutral   Disagree   Strongly Disagree

What I liked best about this staff development program:

What I liked least about this staff development program:

---

person read the current year's staff development plan before meeting to review it. They agreed to evaluate the extent to which needs assessments had been used to establish priorities and select staff development activities.

Linda Novelli reported that Mr. Swensen had agreed to provide the committee with the needs assessment files for the past 3 years.

Mr. Swensen had telephoned Friday morning to tell Ms. Novelli that he had not had time to locate the needs assessment files. He promised to find them Monday.

Sue Welsch distributed copies of the interview questions she and Phil Klein had drafted earlier in the week. The team added two questions on each list and quibbled about the wording of various questions. Tables 1.3 and 1.4 present the interview protocols.

Steve Green and Jane Chandler circulated copies of the tally sheet (see Table 1.2) they had developed. Green explained that the procedure for determining how many programs had used a needs assessment process was as simple as counting the number of documents in the files and calculating a percentage of total programs offered for the year.

Linda Novelli and Jane Chandler shared the list of questions they had prepared for the program participants' questionnaire. After considerable discussion the team decided that the questions should be grouped in two categories: (1) Program quality and (2) program relevance. The revised version of the questionnaire is presented in Table 1.5.

Keep the Process Moving

When the meeting ended, the evaluation team had a new list of tasks. Linda Novelli agreed to tally the needs assessment results when she received the files from Mr. Swensen. Sue Welsch and Phil Klein agreed to interview the Staff Development Advisory Committee as a group and to interview Mr. Swensen individually. Jane Chandler offered to copy the questionnaire and distribute it to all teachers in the school district who had attended workshops. Because the end of the fall semester was near, they agreed to meet next on January 12th.

A few days later, Jane Chandler met with Mr. Swensen to get program rosters for programs offered during the previous 12 months. After a little rummaging through his file cabinets, Mr. Swensen located the appropriate lists. The district had offered 14 programs, enrolling between 18 and 90 participants. The total number of names on the program roster was 473, but many teachers attended multiple workshops. By eliminating duplicate names, Chandler found 223 teachers qualified to receive questionnaires.

By checking the district's telephone book, Chandler discovered that 27 of the 223 teachers no longer worked with the district. During the 3 days Central Duplicating required to copy the survey, Chandler wrote a cover memorandum and addressed envelopes. The cover memorandum explained the purpose of the survey and asked teachers to return the completed forms to Jane Chandler within 5 working days. Chandler distributed the survey and cover memorandum to 196 teachers through interoffice mail.

TABLE 1.6 Staff Development Program Questionnaire: Data Analysis Summary Sheet

Program Content and Delivery

1. The content of this program was logically organized and presented.

	Frequency	Percentage	Mean
Strongly Agree (5)	21	19.3	3.45
Agree (4)	25	22.9	
Neutral (3)	53	48.6	
Disagree (2)	6	5.5	
Strongly Disagree (1)	4	3.7	
Total	109	100.0	

2. The trainer was well prepared.

	Frequency	Percentage	Mean
Strongly Agree (5)	26	23.9	3.74
Agree (4)	41	37.6	
Neutral (3)	30	27.5	
Disagree (2)	12	11.0	
Strongly Disagree (1)	0	0.0	
Total	109	100.0	

3. The support materials (handouts, overheads, slides, exercises, etc.) were effective.

	Frequency	Percentage	Mean
Strongly Agree (5)	24	22.0	3.72
Agree (4)	47	43.1	
Neutral (3)	21	19.3	
Disagree (2)	17	15.6	
Strongly Disagree (1)	0	0.0	
Total	109	100.0	

Chandler received 54 surveys within the 5 days she had allocated. Dismayed by a 27% response rate, she sent a reminder to everyone on her list, generating 17 more surveys. Still disappointed with a response rate of only 36%, Jane Chandler again mailed the survey and cover memo to the 196 teachers who had attended workshops. In this mailing, she wrote PLEASE in large block letters across the bottom of the memo. This mailing added 38 more surveys. The three attempts produced 109 surveys, for a response rate of 55%.

Tallies of the survey results are presented in Table 1.6. Responses of "Strongly Agree" were rated as "5," "Agree" was rated as "4," "Neutral" was rated as "3," "Disagree was rated as "2," and "Strongly Disagree" was rated as "1." The survey questions about program content and delivery were rated more favorably than were the questions about relevance or usefulness. The responses to Ques-

TABLE 1.6 (Continued)

Program Relevance

4. I learned things in this workshop that I can apply in my classroom.

	Frequency	Percentage	Mean
Strongly Agree (5)	10	9.2	2.61
Agree (4)	12	11.0	
Neutral (3)	17	15.6	
Disagree (2)	50	45.9	
Strongly Disagree (1)	18	16.5	
Total	107	100.0	

5. This program was relevant to problems I face as a teacher.

	Frequency	Percentage	Mean
Strongly Agree (5)	15	13.8	2.62
Agree (4)	12	11.0	
Neutral (3)	13	11.9	
Disagree (2)	55	50.5	
Strongly Disagree (1)	14	12.8	
Total	109	100.0	

6. I am a better teacher because of this workshop.

	Frequency	Percentage	Mean
Strongly Agree (5)	5	4.6	1.74
Agree (4)	4	3.7	
Neutral (3)	1	0.9	
Disagree (2)	47	43.1	
Strongly Disagree (1)	52	47.7	
Total	109	100.0	

---

tions 1, 2, and 3 averaged 3.45, 3.74, and 3.72, respectively. The responses to the first two questions were relatively high, indicating that program content and delivery were more than adequate. The responses to Questions 4, 5, and 6 averaged 2.61, 2.62, and 1.74, respectively. These lower scores indicated that the workshops were not regarded as practical or relevant.

On January 12th the evaluation team met to analyze the annual staff development plan and discuss other evaluation issues. The team concluded that the plan was well organized, well written, and accurately described the staff development activities scheduled for the current year. The plan, however, contained no list of priorities, no unifying theme, and no needs analysis as justification for the staff development activities planned for the year.

At this meeting Linda Novelli reported that over a 3-week period she had repeatedly asked Mr. Swensen for files containing the needs assessment analyses. Mr. Swensen finally told Novelli that he simply could not find the files. When pressed, he told her that few formal needs assessments had been conducted. He went on to say that he relied on his judgment and the advice of the Staff Development Advisory Committee to set priorities and choose programs.

Working as a team, Welsch and Klein interviewed both the Staff Development Advisory Committee and Mr. Swensen. Using the interview protocol developed earlier, Sue Welsch asked the questions and Phil Klein made notes. When the answers were unclear or a disagreement emerged among committee members, either Welsch or Klein would probe for more information or ask a follow-up question, being careful to remain neutral with their probes. After interviewing both Mr. Swensen and the committee, Welsch and Klein compared the two sets of notes, looking for consistencies and inconsistencies.

Mr. Swensen and the committee agreed on most questions. They did not agree, however, on the role the committee played in setting priorities and selecting programs. The committee thought that Mr. Swensen set priorities and selected most of the programs, but Mr. Swensen saw their role as significant. Mr. Swensen believed that committee members regularly polled teachers and principals before providing advice on staff development issues. The committee members, however, said that they rarely discussed staff development issues with other teachers or with their principals.

Mr. Swensen and the committee agreed that he would write the annual staff development plan after discussing the broad outlines of the next year's program with the committee. Both the committee and Mr. Swensen were satisfied with this arrangement, and both thought the committee was effective. Neither Mr. Swensen nor the committee recommended any major changes in the way they operated.

Interpreting the Data

Understanding Your Findings

In early February the evaluation team met to discuss the information gathered. They organized the information according to the three evaluation questions identified at the beginning of the project.

1. Is there a systematic plan for the staff development activities conducted each year?

   By studying the annual staff development plan, the team concluded that staff development activities were offered in an orderly manner according to a well-established schedule. Although the plan was systematic, the team was not satisfied that the plan was responsive to the needs of teachers.

2. Are the staff development coordinator and the Staff Development Advisory Committee using needs assessment procedures to determine which programs to offer?

The team had to conclude that needs assessment was not used to determine which programs to offer. There was no evidence of the use of needs assessment in developing the annual staff development plan. Mr. Swensen had been unable to find any of the needs assessment reports requested, and the Staff Development Advisory Committee had appeared to be puzzled by the term *needs assessment* when interviewed by Welsch and Klein.

3. Do teachers have systematic input into the staff development programs offered?

The evidence for this question came from the survey of program participants. The survey results suggested that the quality of the program was high in terms of content and instructor performance. The survey also suggested that the programs were not very relevant to teachers' immediate classroom needs. Reading the comments on the survey questionnaires returned, the team discovered that the district-wide approach to staff development was the primary problem. The questionnaire results supported the argument that teachers considered most staff development programs to be of little relevance to their work.

On any given "in-service" day, the district would offer a single workshop or activity for all teachers in the district. If the program was general enough for all, it lacked specific application to the classroom. If the program was specific to a given subject area or grade level, it was irrelevant to most of those attending the workshop.

Changes Resulting From the Evaluation

Benefits From Evaluation

During the last week in February, the evaluation team met with Superintendent Skidmore. They provided her with a four-page report of their evaluation. The report concluded with the following recommendations:

1. Develop and use a formal needs assessment procedure to set staff development priorities and to select programs.
2. Adopt a school-focused staff development plan. Offer staff development programs customized to meet the needs of the teachers in particular schools.
3. Make certain that the staff development committee members understand that their primary responsibility is to discover the staff development needs of teachers and to communicate those needs to Mr. Swensen, the Staff Development Coordinator.
4. Give school principals a larger role in establishing staff development priorities for their schools.

After listening to the evaluation team, Ms. Skidmore asked them to organize a presentation of their findings and recommendations for

Mr. Swensen and the Staff Development Advisory Committee. On behalf of the evaluation team, Linda Novelli accepted the request.

Linda Novelli met with Mr. Swensen to arrange the presentation. At that meeting she provided Mr. Swensen with a copy of the evaluation team's report and its four recommendations. She tried to assure him that the report and recommendations were not an attack on him. To Novelli's surprise, Mr. Swensen agreed that the evaluation was "probably" accurate and that the recommendations were "sensible." They scheduled the presentation to the Staff Development Advisory Committee for the second week in March.

Mr. Swensen and all members of the Staff Development Advisory Committee attended the presentation. The presentation of results from the survey of teachers generated the most discussion. The Advisory Committee expressed shock about the teachers' negative responses to the staff development programs offered.

Novelli spent considerable time explaining that even a "good" staff development program could be irrelevant. After considerable discussion, Mr. Swensen suggested that he and the committee wanted to develop an action plan for improving the district's staff development programs. He said that the evaluation team's work would guide him and the committee in devising the action plan.

Summary of Evaluation Principles

This vignette illustrated several principles that are useful in evaluating school staff development programs:

1. A focus for the evaluation was clearly established. The committee determined the scope of the evaluation, formulated specific evaluation questions, reached agreement about the expected finished product, and determined the resources necessary to complete the task.

2. The evaluation committee was composed of a variety of individuals with an interest in staff development. This ensures that the interests of various stakeholders are protected.

3. Where possible, the evaluation committee collected data by taking a census. A census gives you more accurate results than a sample and is preferred over a sample unless it is too costly to take a census.

4. When the committee identified a program weakness, action was taken to overcome the weakness. This is consistent with the formative approach to evaluation.

5. Whenever possible, the evaluation team sought at least two ways of obtaining the same information. In this case, the evaluation committee examined both the annual staff development plan and asked for needs assessment reports to determine how priorities

were established. In addition, the committee collected data from teachers.

6. The data needed for the evaluation were systematically collected, tabulated, and analyzed.

7. The results of the evaluation were presented in a systematic, organized fashion in a written report. This written record will make it possible for other evaluators to build on the work of this team. The written report also makes it possible for others to assess the rigor of the research of this evaluation team.

Alternative Strategies

Other Approaches The evaluation team could have used several other approaches in conducting their assessment. The teacher surveys could have been supplemented with interviews or focus groups that might have produced more and richer data. If more than one source of information supports a conclusion, the evaluation team can have greater confidence in the validity of its findings.

Principals are important stakeholders in the staff development process, but no information was collected from them systematically. The team could have easily surveyed or interviewed principals about their roles in setting staff development priorities. With the principals' opinions supporting those of the teachers, the evaluation team's recommendations would have been even more compelling.

Cautions Regarding Misinterpretations

The problems in this vignette seem obvious. Getting teachers involved in setting priorities also seems an obvious solution. A staff development program based solely on the ideas of teachers, however, may also have problems. At times the staff development coordinator should champion priorities that could not win the immediate support of teachers.

National professional associations and accrediting bodies frequently endorse causes not immediately embraced by most teachers. Occasionally, research findings may highlight appropriate new directions for staff development programs. In these cases, teachers may not be the best judges of their own needs.

2 Vignette Two

The Use of Staff Development Advisory Committees

Background Dr. Janet Lawson, Superintendent of the Livingstone School District, asked William Harwood, Principal of Chesapeake Middle School, to serve as chairperson of the district's Staff Development Evaluation Committee. Dr. Lawson explained that the ad hoc task force would be responsible for determining how well the district's Staff Development Advisory Committee was functioning. When Harwood asked her why the task force was necessary, Lawson responded that she had heard "some rumbling and grumbling" from people who had served on the committee in recent years. Lawson's charge to the evaluation committee was to study the structure and functioning of the Staff Development Advisory Committee.

The evaluation committee consisted of six people—four teachers, a counselor, and the staff development coordinator. Mr. Harwood, a high school English teacher with 8 years of experience, had served on a number of district-wide committees, chairing two of them. He had worked closely with the staff development coordinator to pick hard-working committee members who were knowledgeable about staff development activities. Two of the teachers on the committee were high school teachers, one was a middle school teacher, and one was an elementary school teacher. The counselor was from Wharton Middle School.

Focusing the Evaluation

Given the specific nature of the evaluation committee's charge, their attention was immediately focused on the Staff Development Advisory Committee. The superintendent appoints members of the Staff Development Advisory Committee and supervises the staff development coordinator. The evaluation team focused on assessing the effectiveness of the district's Staff Development Advisory Committee.

Use of Standards and Indicators of Quality

One of the standards in Resource A of this guide addresses the purpose and function of a school system's staff development advisory committee. The standard is:

> **Standard 3:** *Advisory Committee.* The school or school system should have a staff development advisory committee that encourages participation by all parties involved in staff development activities.

Two indicators of quality were identified for this standard:

3.1. The school should have, or have representation on, a formal committee or other body responsible for the development, delivery, and monitoring of staff development activities.

3.2. The staff development advisory committee should have wide representation from the faculty, staff, and administration of the school.

After a brief discussion, the evaluation team decided that the standard was both sensible and straightforward. In fact, one of the team members quipped, "So what's to evaluate? We know we've got one. So let's go home."

They also agreed that the first indicator of quality—the existence of a formal committee with responsibility for planning and monitoring staff development activities—was an appropriate way to judge the scope of responsibilities of the Staff Development Advisory Committee. The second indicator was regarded as a precursor of the responsiveness of the advisory committee to important stakeholders.

Data Collection and Analysis

Clarification of Issues

The evaluation task force discussed Standard 3 at some length and concluded that two key issues needed to be addressed. The first issue was the structure of the advisory committee. The task force

TABLE 2.1 An Explanation of the Criteria Used to Appoint Members of the Staff Development Advisory Committee

Memorandum

To: Mr. William Harwood, Chairperson
      Staff Development Evaluation Committee

From: Dr. Janet Lawson, Superintendent
      Livingstone School District

RE: Criteria for Membership on the Staff Development Advisory Committee

As you know, the Staff Development Advisory Committee is an extremely important committee for this school district. The work of this committee directly influences the quality of the education offered to students in this district. Consequently, we must have people of the highest caliber on this committee. We also want people on the committee to be broadly representative of the school community. With these factors in mind, I ask each principal to nominate someone from his or her school to be on the advisory committee. I then write to the person nominated asking him or her to serve on the advisory committee. I also appoint at least two principals or assistant principals to the committee.

I hope this information has been helpful, and I look forward to your full report soon.

decided to determine if the advisory committee fairly represented the schools in the district.

Mr. Harwood wrote a letter to Dr. Janet Lawson, Superintendent of Livingstone School District, asking for an explanation of the criteria used to appoint members of the Staff Development Advisory Committee. Within a week the committee received a memo from Dr. Lawson (see Table 2.1).

The evaluation committee decided that the best way to get the information needed concerning the functioning of the advisory committee was to conduct interviews with the committee's members. The interviews were divided up, so that no one had to interview more than three members of the Staff Development Advisory Committee. Because some of the crucial questions to be asked concerned the relationship between the committee and the staff development coordinator, the evaluation committee decided that it would be inappropriate for the staff development coordinator to interview advisory committee members. Mr. Harwood wrote a letter to each member of the Staff Development Advisory Committee explaining the work of the evaluation committee and asking for cooperation in granting interviews.

TABLE 2.2 Interview Protocol: Staff Development Advisory Committee Members

1. How long have you been on the Staff Development Advisory Committee?
2. Do you see yourself as a representative of a particular group of people in your role as a committee member?
3. What have been the advisory committee's major accomplishments since you have been a member?
4. From your perspective, what are the major duties of the committee?
5. How would you describe the advisory committee's role in producing the annual staff development plan that must be submitted to the state's Department of Education for approval?
6. How would you describe your personal role in producing the annual staff development plan?
7. How would you describe the relationship between the Staff Development Advisory Committee and the staff development coordinator?
8. What, if anything, would you like to see changed about the Staff Development Advisory Committee and the way it functions?
9. Is there anything else you would like to tell the Staff Development Evaluation Committee?

Training for Data Collection

Before conducting the interviews, Mr. Harwood conducted an informal interviewing training session. The following major points were stressed:

1. Stick to the questions on the interview protocol.

   The interviewer should ask all the questions listed on the interview protocol (see Table 2.2). The questions should be asked in the order in which they are listed. Do not get creative and make up your own questions as you go along. This will introduce inconsistency into the data collected from different interviewees.

2. If the first response to a question is unclear or does not clearly answer the question, ask a follow-up question that probes the original question.

   Effective probes include:
   - Could you elaborate on that?
   - Could you say more about that?
   - How is that?
   - In what way?
   - How would you explain that?
   - I'm not sure I'm following you.
   - What do you mean?
   - Why?

- Um-huh . . .
- Silence

3. The questions should be asked in a neutral tone of voice.

It is important to get the interviewee's true opinion. If the interviewer reveals his or her own attitude about the appropriate answer to the questions posed, many interviewees will respond with answers they believe the interviewer wants to hear. Similarly, the interviewer should not respond either positively or negatively to answers given by the interviewee.

4. The interview should be conducted in a formal, structured, professional manner.

Although it is appropriate to spend a few minutes informally establishing rapport before an interview begins, the interview itself should be a formal, structured exchange, guided by the interview protocol. This may be somewhat difficult in a small district where everyone is well acquainted with everyone else, but an interview should not be an informal chat.

5. Take notes as the interviewee talks.

Even though it is somewhat awkward to write while someone is talking, you cannot trust your memory to reconstruct the answers to your questions later. After the interview, you may want to rewrite your notes, adding comments you could not get down quickly enough during the interview. With the interviewee's permission, you may wish to record the interview. Remember, however, that an interviewee is likely to be less candid if a tape recorder is used.

6. Thank the interviewee for taking the time to grant you an interview.

Extending this courtesy to your interviewee increases the likelihood for continued participation in the evaluation process. It also increases the probability that the interviewee will consider the recommendations of the evaluation committee in a positive light.

Use a Standard Approach to Interviews

The training session concluded with several mock interviews, with each committee member taking turns playing the role of interviewer and interviewee. The evaluation committee members used the Interview Protocol presented in Table 2.2 to structure the mock interviews. Mr. Harwood asked the committee members to complete their interviews prior to their next meeting, scheduled a week from hence.

Dealing With Sensitive Issues

About 3 days before the next scheduled meeting, Mr. Harwood received telephone calls from three different committee members. In a different way, each person told him that their findings would upset Ms. Whitehouse, the staff development coordinator. Each also asked if it would be possible to meet without Ms. Whitehouse at the next meeting of the committee. In each case he said he would let them know.

TABLE 2.3 Summary of Interview Results: Interviews of Staff Development Advisory Committee Members

---

1. How long have you been on the Staff Development Advisory Committee?
   - 1 year or less—10
   - 2 years—4 (1 teacher; 1 counselor; 2 assistant principals)
   - 3 years or more—0

2. Do you see yourself as a representative of a particular group of people in your role as a committee member?
   - My school— 9 teachers; 1 counselor
   - Math and Science teachers—1
   - Middle school teachers—1
   - The school district—1 assistant principal
   - No one in particular—1 assistant principal

3. What have been the advisory committee's major accomplishments since you have been a member?
   - Most interviewees had a difficult time with this question, starting out with answers such as, "Well, I'm not too sure." With probing:
       - Completed district's staff development plan—8

4. From your perspective, what are the major duties of the committee?
   - Approve the staff development plan prepared by the staff development coordinator.—8
   - Help the staff development coordinator—3
   - See that there are good staff development programs for math and science teachers—2
   - Well, it's just another committee—1

5. How would you describe the advisory committee's role in producing the annual staff development plan?
   - The staff development coordinator writes the report and we approve it —8
   - Not much—2
   - I'm not sure—4

Mr. Harwood arranged to meet Ms. Lynn Whitehouse, the staff development coordinator, the next day after school. Although he was somewhat nervous and uncomfortable, Mr. Harwood told Ms. Whitehouse that he thought it would be best if the committee met without her when it discussed the results of the interviews with the Staff Development Advisory Committee. She said that she was a little bit surprised, but that she understood.

Mr. Harwood entered the next committee meeting later that week with some trepidation. He had asked each person on the evaluation committee to bring enough copies of their completed interview protocols to share with everyone else on the committee. After these

TABLE 2.3 (Continued)

---

6. How would you describe your personal role in producing the annual staff development plan?
   - None—12
   - I'm not sure—2

7. How would you describe the relationship between the Staff Development Advisory Committee and the staff development coordinator?
   - The staff development coordinator is too bossy—3
   - Too little involvement on the part of the committee—7
   - Positive—1 assistant principal
   - Efficient and effective—1 assistant principal

8. What, if anything, would you like to see changed about the Staff Development Advisory Committee and the way it functions?
   - More involvement by more members of the committee—10
   - I would like to get off the committee —2
   - Get a new staff development coordinator—2

9. Is there anything else you would like to tell the Staff Development Evaluation Committee?
   - Keep up the good work—2 assistant principals
   - Tell Ms. Whitehouse not to be so opinionated and bossy—2
   - Have the superintendent come to some of our meetings to see what goes on—1
   - Train the staff development coordinator to run a meeting in a participative way—1
   - No—8

---

had been distributed, he asked the evaluation committee members to spend a few minutes silently reading the documents before discussing them.

After everyone had finished reading the interview protocols, Mr. Harwood asked the committee to divide up into two groups to work on summarizing the interview results. The first group summarized Questions 1 through 4, and the second group summarized Questions 5 through 8. To summarize the responses to a question, one person read all responses aloud while the rest of the group classified each response into a summary category. The results of this procedure are presented in Table 2.3.

Interpretation of the Results

After summarizing the data, the evaluation committee took only 10 minutes to reach a consensus about the meaning of the interviews.

TABLE 2.4 Strengths of the Staff Development Advisory Committee

- The committee is appropriately representative of the
  various types of schools—Elementary schools, middle schools,
  and high schools are represented on the committee.

- The committee is balanced in terms of race, gender,
  and age.

- The committee is balanced in terms of disciplines and
  specialties—Math, science, English, social studies, counseling,
  and special education interests are represented on the committee.

- The committee is representative of school district
  staff, with the membership including teachers, counselors, and
  administrators.

All of the teachers on the Staff Development Advisory Committee regarded the committee as a frustrating waste of time, but the two assistant principals thought the committee was well organized and effective. Both groups were convinced that Ms. Whitehouse was responsible for the current state of affairs.

Specific complaints from the teachers were:

- The committee meetings run too long.
- Ms. Whitehouse does all the talking.
- The advisory committee doesn't really advise. Ms. Whitehouse does all the committee's work herself and simply expects members to agree with her conclusions.
- One teacher said that he did not know why he was on the committee, unless it was some kind of punishment from his principal.

The assistant principals on the committee indicated:

- Meetings run efficiently: Ms. Whitehouse comes prepared, gets started on time, and sticks to her agenda.
- Ms. Whitehouse knows the direction the staff development program should take and is organized to accomplish her goals.

Mr. Harwood and the evaluation task force had collected data that suggested serious problems with the functioning of the Staff Development Advisory Committee. Because Ms. Whitehouse was a member of the evaluation committee and the source of at least some of the problems with the Staff Development Advisory Committee, the members of the evaluation committee felt uncomfortable confronting Ms. Whitehouse with the problems.

Jennifer Stevens, an assistant principal at Clayton High School, reminded the committee that they were involved in formative, not

TABLE 2.5 Strengths of the Staff Development Coordinator

- The meeting agendas are distributed ahead of time and closely followed.

- The staff development coordinator is well prepared for each meeting of the advisory committee.

- The staff development plan is prepared on time and presented clearly and coherently by the staff development coordinator.

- The staff development plan is competently prepared and meets the approval of the state Department of Education.

- The administrators on the committee value the staff development coordinator's efficiency in running meetings and gaining approval for the annual staff development plan.

---

summative, evaluation. Their job as evaluators was not to pass final judgment but to find ways to solve problems and make improvements. Formative evaluation seeks to provide guidance in overcoming weaknesses and building on strengths. Ms. Stevens suggested that they start by discussing the strengths of the Staff Development Advisory Committee and Ms. Whitehouse's efforts to work with the committee.

The task force developed two lists of strengths to establish a context for discussing the weaknesses of the Staff Development Advisory Committee. One list (see Table 2.4) focused on the strengths of the Staff Development Advisory Committee, and the other list (see Table 2.5) focused on the strengths of the staff development coordinator working with the advisory committee. With these lists of strengths to provide some perspective, the evaluation team members were less intimidated about confronting Ms. Whitehouse.

A Focus on Improvement   The evaluation committee met with Ms. Whitehouse to share the findings from its interviews with members of the Staff Development Advisory Committee. Mr. Harwood started with a summary of the findings. Emphasizing the positive points first, he told Ms. Whitehouse that the advisory committee was always impressed with the quality of the staff development plan, how hard she worked, and how well-organized she was. However, he said, there were problems.

The problems concerned the degree of participation the advisory committee had in assessing needs, planning programs, monitoring results, and evaluating staff development courses. He told her that the Staff Development Advisory Committee would like to have more involvement in formulating the annual staff development plan. They did not like simply to approve or disapprove a plan developed and written without their help and guidance.

Ms. Whitehouse said she was very surprised by the advisory committee's reaction. She was just trying to make their lives easier by taking care of things. She said that she had not realized that they wanted to be involved to any great extent, because several of the advisory committee members had complained about being assigned to the committee without being asked first. She said that she thought she would be able to work with the Staff Development Advisory Committee in a more open, participative manner. In fact, she welcomed the opportunity to share some of the burden with them.

Interpretation of Results and Problem Solving

Before preparing its final report, the evaluation committee met with the Staff Development Advisory Committee to discuss its findings and tentative conclusions. At the beginning of the meeting Harwood distributed the interview results and copies of the two lists of strengths.

From Findings to Recommendations

After giving them time to read the materials, Harwood asked them to comment on the accuracy of the evaluation task force's description of the relationship between Ms. Whitehouse and the advisory committee. The discussion started slowly, but the advisory committee agreed with the findings. Reaching this consensus, Mr. Harwood said that the evaluation team's job was to recommend ways to strengthen the role and effectiveness of the Staff Development Advisory Committee. Then Mr. Harwood distributed a list of proposed recommendations:

- Development of a more participative format for the functioning of the Staff Development Advisory Committee
- Greater involvement of the Staff Development Advisory Committee in needs assessment, program design, monitoring programs, and evaluating programs
- A larger role for the Staff Development Advisory Committee in preparing the annual staff development plan submitted to the state Department of Education
- A greater degree of delegation from the staff development coordinator to the Staff Development Advisory Committee
- Changes in the process of selecting and assigning members to the Staff Development Advisory Committee to ensure that those appointed to the committee were interested in and committed to staff development

Sandy Wilson was the first person to speak after Mr. Harwood had presented the recommendations. She agreed with the recommendations presented, but said she would like to add one of her own. She suggested that someone other than Ms. Whitehouse should serve as chairperson of the Staff Development Advisory Committee. The new structure, she said, would show that the committee was advisory to rather than subordinate to the staff development coordinator. Others added their support for the recommendation.

At the close of the meeting, Mr. Harwood thanked the group for its cooperation and told them that he would circulate a draft of the team's report approximately a week before its formal release. He encouraged them to read the draft report and to forward suggested changes to him.

The evaluation team, including Ms. Whitehouse, met with the superintendent when the final report was complete. All of the recommendations listed above were included in the final report. The team explained that more time and care needed to go into selecting and orienting members of the Staff Development Advisory Committee. If handled more carefully, the assignment would be regarded as an honor rather than a burden. Superintendent Lawson endorsed the recommendations and changed the procedures for the upcoming school year.

Summary of Evaluation Principles

1. The superintendent selected a credible team leader, someone with a number of years in the district and considerable experience chairing committees.

2. The evaluation was tightly focused. The evaluation questions were carefully selected based on a perceived problem and guided by standards and indicators of quality.

3. The evaluation team matched the data collection device (face-to-face interviews) with the evaluation questions to be answered. The interview is an appropriate data collection tool because it is flexible and sophisticated enough to collect complex, sensitive information.

4. Interviewers were carefully trained and systematic data collection was ensured by using a well-designed interview protocol.

5. The evaluation team involved the advisory committee and the staff development coordinator in the interpretation of the data and in formulation of recommendations.

6. The evaluation was appropriately formative, concentrating on improving the performance of the Staff Development Advisory Committee.

Alternative Strategies

Other Approaches   This particular evaluation focused on the staff development coordinator and the Staff Development Advisory Committee. The interviews discovered problems between the advisory committee and the coordinator. Another approach might have examined how teachers were selected for the committee and how they were oriented or trained for the task. That approach would have concentrated on interviewing principals and perhaps the staff development coordinator.

Cautions Regarding Misinterpretation

The advisory committee members complained about their limited roles in devising the district's staff development plan. The evaluation team assumed that the problem was caused by the staff development coordinator. It may well have been that the advisory committee was less effective than it should have been. The evaluation team gathered no evidence about the competence of the people on the advisory committee. By their own admission they were unclear about their responsibilities as members of the committee. It is possible that the staff development coordinator was compensating for the passive response of committee members.

3

Vignette Three

Adult Learning Theory and the Staff Development Process

Background The principal of Ravenswood Elementary School, Wanda Vines, has just formed a committee to evaluate staff development programs at her school. There was no external pressure to do an evaluation, but she thought that the general quality of staff development programs could be improved. Recently, she overhead a group of teachers complaining about the "Mickey Mouse" approach used by some of the staff development trainers the district had employed. The committee is composed of three teachers, the school's three best teachers in her opinion. Ms. Vines chaired the committee herself.

First Team Meeting

Focusing the Evaluation At the first meeting of the evaluation committee, Ms. Vines voiced the overheard complaints and asked if those complaints pointed to serious problems. At one point in the ensuing discussion, a teacher complained that they were treated like children by the staff development trainers. One of the teachers, Juanita Reyes, commented that one of the courses she was taking as part of her master's degree program at Lancaster State University was exploring the concept of adult learning theory. The committee showed great interest in exploring whether or not staff development programs could be improved by

47

hiring trainers who used the principles of adult learning theory. Ms. Reyes volunteered to prepare some background material for the next meeting of the committee.

At the next meeting, Ms. Reyes distributed copies of articles on adult learning theory and staff development from the *Journal of Staff Development*. After some discussion, the members of the committee agreed that many of the district's staff development trainers treated the participants as passive, immature children rather than as active, mature adults.

Use of Standards and Indicators of Quality

They agreed that the evaluation committee should concentrate on assessing how well staff development trainers used the principles of adult learning theory to guide their teaching. Consulting Resource A of this guide, committee members found that Standard 7 addressed the competence and performance of staff development trainers. One of the indicators specifically addressed the need for staff development trainers to use adult learning theory in their programs and activities. The evaluation committee decided to assess that indicator during the upcoming school year.

> **Standard 7:** *Staff Development Trainers.* The staff development trainers should be highly competent and have the background and experiences necessary to give them high credibility with program participants.

> Indicator 7.4. Trainers should have a demonstrated knowledge of adult learning theory.

The adult learning theory indicator was only one of six indicators that could be used to assess staff development trainers. The evaluation committee decided to focus on a single indicator for the current year, because limited resources made it impractical to assess performance on every indicator simultaneously.

Developing and Using Data Collection Instruments

The committee decided to collect background material on staff development practices and adult learning theory. One Saturday spent in the library at Lancaster State produced a number of articles on adult learning theory and staff development. The Summer 1988 issue of the *Journal of Staff Development* proved particularly helpful, with the entire issue devoted to adult learning theory.

Potential Information Sources

A number of potential sources and data collection strategies were suggested for collecting data on Indicator 7.4. The committee decided to devise a questionnaire to be completed by program participants (see Table 3.1). The questionnaire was designed to ask program participants to rate the extent to which various characteristics of adult learning theory were present in staff development programs or activities they had attended. After reviewing a number of articles on adult learning theory, the committee made a list of behaviors, attitudes, and practices that were consistent with adult learning theory.

The questionnaire they designed used a Likert-type scale. Each statement on the questionnaire made a statement about the staff development activity, and respondents were asked to rate the extent to which they agreed or disagreed with each statement.

The evaluation committee had the participants complete questionnaires for each of six staff development programs offered to the staff of their elementary school during the academic year. The questionnaire was completed as the final task of each of the staff development programs. In all cases, a member of the evaluation committee distributed and collected the questionnaires. The questionnaires were completed while the staff development trainer was out of the room.

The data were tallied and summarized using the data collection sheets presented in Table 3.1. The committee calculated the frequency and percentage of each response, and the mean and standard deviation for each item on the questionnaire. The results for one staff development program, Fostering Self-Confidence in Learning Disabled Children, is presented in Table 3.2. For scoring purposes, each item marked Strongly Agree received a score of "1," each item marked Agree received a score of "2," each item marked Neutral received a score of "3," each item marked Disagree received a score of "4," and each item marked Strongly Disagree received a score of "5."

Interpreting and Applying the Data

Understanding the Findings

Over the course of the year, the committee collected and analyzed the data on each of its staff development programs. The questionnaire results cast some doubts on the use of adult learning theory to teach the workshop titled Fostering Self-Confidence in Learning Disabled Children. The trainer received relatively high scores on stimulating problem solving, generating internal motivation, making good use of the participants' prior experience, and providing opportunities for self-development. The results were mixed for items related to encouraging active participation, stimulating collaboration, and demonstrating respect for program participants. The lowest scores were for delivering material with practical applicability and allowing participants to influence course content and manner of presentation.

TABLE 3.1 Staff Development Program Questionnaire

Program Name _____   Instructor _____

INSTRUCTIONS: Please rate the staff development program you have just completed on each of the items listed below. There are no right or wrong responses to the statements listed below. Circle the response that most closely describes your opinion concerning the item. Do not put your name on this form. All responses are anonymous and confidential.

1. Instruction was characterized by respect for program participants.

   Strongly Agree   Agree   Neutral   Disagree   Strongly Disagree

2. The trainer involved the participants as active collaborators in the educational experience.

   Strongly Agree   Agree   Neutral   Disagree   Strongly Disagree

3. This staff development activity provided ample opportunity for self-development.

   Strongly Agree   Agree   Neutral   Disagree   Strongly Disagree

4. This program failed to make good use of the prior experience of program participants.

   Strongly Agree   Agree   Neutral   Disagree   Strongly Disagree

5. This program fostered active participation in the learning process by program participants.

   Strongly Agree   Agree   Neutral   Disagree   Strongly Disagree

6. This program discouraged problem solving on the part of program participants.

   Strongly Agree   Agree   Neutral   Disagree   Strongly Disagree

7. This program emphasized learning things that had immediate application to my job.

   Strongly Agree   Agree   Neutral   Disagree   Strongly Disagree

8. The staff development trainer stressed the importance of internal motivation for mastering the concepts and skills offered by this program.

   Strongly Agree   Agree   Neutral   Disagree   Strongly Disagree

9. This program did not respond to my needs for professional growth and development.

   Strongly Agree   Agree   Neutral   Disagree   Strongly Disagree

10. I was given an opportunity to influence the content and presentation of this staff development course or activity.

    Strongly Agree   Agree   Neutral   Disagree   Strongly Disagree

The committee regarded these results as "disappointing" but not unacceptable. Of the other five courses evaluated during the year, this particular trainer taught two. The results just presented were for the first course. After the first course, Ms. Vines shared the results with the trainer, who was surprised at how low some of the scores were. Ms. Vines shared several articles on adult learning theory with the trainer, and he used these to modify his approach to the workshop. When he taught his second workshop, the ratings on the same questionnaire were substantially higher.

Summary of Evaluation Principles Illustrated in This Vignette

1. Focus the evaluation on an area that is sufficiently limited in scope to be accomplished in the time given. The committee did not try to evaluate all aspects of the performance of the staff development trainers. They concentrated on the use of adult learning theory in the design and delivery of staff development programs.

2. Questionnaire design was based on concepts defined in the professional literature on staff development. It is much more likely that a self-designed questionnaire will measure the variables of interest if the questions are closely related to the definitions, concepts, and constructs presented in the professional literature.

3. Some of the questionnaire items were stated positively and some were stated negatively. Varying the format of the questions asked prevents respondents from giving an identical response to each question without reading and considering the questions first (see *Evaluating School Programs: An Educator's Guide,* by Sanders, in this series).

4. The evaluation committee undertook its work in the spirit of formative development. When the data indicated a problem with a particular staff development trainer, they shared this information with him and encouraged him to incorporate more characteristics of adult learning theory into his instruction. He responded positively, improving his ratings on a subsequent course.

Alternative Strategies

Other Approaches   The approach to evaluation in this vignette used a questionnaire to assess the trainers' use of adult learning theory in the presentation of staff development programs. Another approach would have been observation of workshops by a trained observer using a behavioral observation scale. Trained observers using carefully designed behavioral observation scales can collect highly accurate information.

text continued on p. 54

TABLE 3.2 Staff Development Program Questionnaire: Data Analysis Summary Sheet

Program: Fostering Self-Confidence in Learning Disabled Children

Instructor: Tom Wolfe

1. Instruction was characterized by respect for program participants.

	Frequency	Percentage	Mean
Strongly Agree	3	11	2.82
Agree	11	39	
Neutral	3	11	
Disagree	10	36	
Strongly Disagree	1	3	
Total	28	100	

2. The trainer involved participants as active collaborators in the educational experience.

	Frequency	Percentage	Mean
Strongly Agree	3	13	2.42
Agree	14	58	
Neutral	4	17	
Disagree	2	8	
Strongly Disagree	1	4	
Total	24	100	

3. This staff development activity provided ample opportunity for self-development.

	Frequency	Percentage	Mean
Strongly Agree	7	25	2.00
Agree	16	57	
Neutral	3	11	
Disagree	2	7	
Strongly Disagree	0	0	
Total	28	100	

4. This program failed to make good use of the prior experience of program participants.

	Frequency	Percentage	Mean
Strongly Agree	0	0	4.18
Agree	0	0	
Neutral	4	14	
Disagree	19	68	
Strongly Disagree	5	18	
Total	28	100	

TABLE 3.2 (Continued)

5. This program fostered active participation in the learning process by program participants.

	Frequency	Percentage	Mean
Strongly Agree	6	21	3.25
Agree	10	36	
Neutral	11	39	
Disagree	1	4	
Strongly Disagree	0	0	
Total	28	100	

6. This program discouraged problem solving on the part of program participants.

	Frequency	Percentage	Mean
Strongly Agree	0	0	4.18
Agree	0	0	
Neutral	4	14	
Disagree	19	68	
Strongly Disagree	5	18	
Total	28	100	

7. The program emphasized learning things that had immediate application to my job.

	Frequency	Percentage	Mean
Strongly Agree	3	11	3.57
Agree	4	14	
Neutral	3	11	
Disagree	10	36	
Strongly Disagree	8	28	
Total	28	100	

8. The staff development trainer stressed the importance of internal motivation for mastering the concepts and skills offered by this program.

	Frequency	Percentage	Mean
Strongly Agree	7	25	3.96
Agree	15	56	
Neutral	4	15	
Disagree	1	4	
Strongly Disagree	0	0	
Total	27	100	

continued

TABLE 3.2 (Continued)

9. This program did not respond to my needs for professional growth and development.

	Frequency	Percentage	Mean
Strongly Agree	0	0	4.18
Agree	0	0	
Neutral	4	14	
Disagree	19	68	
Strongly Disagree	5	18	
Total	28	100	

10. I was able to have influence on the content and presentation of this staff development course or activity.

	Frequency	Percentage	Mean
Strongly Agree	3	11	3.46
Agree	5	17	
Neutral	3	11	
Disagree	10	36	
Strongly Disagree	7	25	
Total	28	100	

NOTE: Strongly Agree = 1; Strongly Disagree = 5.

The evaluation team could have interviewed or surveyed the staff development trainers concerning teaching philosophies and techniques. This approach would have been a more direct way to assess how much the trainers understood and endorsed adult learning theory. This approach has the advantage of measuring rather than inferring the trainers' knowledge of and commitment to adult learning theory. Information about a trainer's knowledge of adult learn theory may not, however, reveal how skillfully he or she translates philosophy into practice.

Cautions Regarding Misinterpretation

Information regarding trainers' use of adult learning theory was collected with a short questionnaire designed by the evaluation team. It would be unwise to trust this questionnaire to measure the adult learning theory construct with a high degree of accuracy. More confidence could be placed in the results if the team had used more than one source of information. Data from interviews or focus groups would have strengthened the conclusions of the evaluation team.

4

Vignette Four

Evaluating Staff Development Workshops for At-Risk Students

Background **J**o Mitchell, Staff Development Coordinator for Manson Park School District, met with principals in her school district in early March to begin discussion of staff development needs for the upcoming school year. She suggested to the principals that the district conduct a "needs assessment" linked to the state's "cycle for school improvement."

Each year the state Department of Education identified several major themes for improving the functioning of schools. Frequently, special materials and seed funding were available from the state for promoting improvement in targeted areas. The themes targeted for the coming year included computational skills, foreign language instruction, site-based management programs, and curriculum development aimed at improving the performance of students.

School Problems Point to Staff Development Needs Gus Beaumont, principal of Parc Glynn Elementary School, asked, "Do we have to stick with State's list of themes?"

"No, but there are more resources available to us if we do," answered Ms. Mitchell. "What alternative theme did you have in mind?"

"Well, I don't know, but it seems we should do something that relates directly to our own problems."

"We have a lot of problems. Which ones do you have in mind?" responded Mitchell.

"How about the attendance problems we have with the kids of migrant workers?" Gus responded.

"It's not just attendance," added Elaine Gibson, assistant principal at Parc Glynn. "Many of those same students have trouble with English. They speak Spanish at home and a mixture of Spanish and English at school."

"It's not just the children of migrant workers who have language problems. Somewhere between 30% and 35% of the students at Melrose speak English as a second language. I'll bet the percentage is almost as high district-wide. In addition to Spanish, we have significant numbers of students whose first language is Chinese, Cambodian, Vietnamese, Russian, French, or Hungarian. There's also a smattering of other languages. Some of these students are very proficient in English, some struggle, and others are completely lost," said Tanya Greene, principal of Melrose.

"True, language can be a problem, but I'm more concerned with our students who are on the road to trouble, both academically and personally. We have kids in this district who come from very poor families. Usually, these are single-parent families headed by women who aren't at home when school lets out because they have to work. There's frequently not enough money for after-school care, so many of these kids are unsupervised after school. Unsupervised, they not only don't do their homework, but may be out on the streets exposed to crime, drugs, and gangs. These kids are just as big a problem—or bigger—than the kids with language problems."

"While we're talking about problems, let's recognize that many of our students drop out each year because they become pregnant," remarked Tanya Greene.

With this last comment, Jo Mitchell chuckled, "As I said, we certainly have our share of problems. From listening to your comments, I can see a way to respond to our specific problems and still participate in the statewide funding. Almost all of the problems you have voiced increase the student's chances of failing academically or dropping out of school. You are really discussing the problems that put students at risk of failing, and staff development programs focused on 'at-risk' students is one of the funding priorities for the year. It sounds as if we can have our cake and eat it too on this one."

"What do you mean?" asked Gus Beaumont.

"Well, the problems we have been discussing are local problems, right?"

"Right," answered Beaumont.

"Taken together these issues constitute the factors that put students at risk for academic failure. Right?" asked Mitchell.

"Right."

"So why can't we design staff development programs for the year that address some, if not all, of these issues under the umbrella of efforts to improve the success of at-risk students?"

"I see what you mean. That sounds like a good idea," Gus Beaumont responded.

Jo Mitchell asked the rest of the group what they thought. The response was favorable, and they set about outlining what they wanted from a staff development program for at-risk students. By the end of the meeting they had decided that they would like to have a staff development program that would teach classroom teachers to identify which children were at risk and to devise a specific strategy aimed at helping a particular student.

They also decided to survey classroom teachers to see if they thought a staff development program focused on at-risk students would be helpful. Jo Mitchell agreed to poll teachers to see if they responded positively to the idea of an at-risk staff development program. In the course of the next week, Ms. Mitchell telephoned 15 teachers in four different schools to talk to them about the possibility of staff development workshops that would increase the teacher's ability to identify and work with at-risk students. Nine of the teachers responded enthusiastically, 2 were very negative, and the other 4 were either somewhat positive or neutral. Based on this response, Ms. Mitchell decided to go ahead with the proposed topic.

Designing a Staff Development Program

For the next meeting of the staff development committee, Jo Mitchell invited three teachers to join the group. As the meeting began, she distributed the materials she had obtained from the state education office on conducting staff development workshops for teachers that concerned at-risk students. The topics covered by the materials sent from the state education office included dealing with truancy, responding to the needs of the developmentally disabled, in-school suspension programs, self-esteem workshops for students, establishing an alternative high school for students who had already dropped out, and peer tutoring programs. Also included were a workbook called *Quick Help for At-Risk Students: A Teacher's Guide,* and a checklist called "Identifying the Risk Factors for Dropouts."

After looking at the material, one of the teachers, Wanda Stratton, commented that there was "way too much stuff" to do in one year's worth of workshops. Either the range of topics needed to be pared down or something other than the regular staff development workshops was going to be needed. The other teachers agreed that there seemed to be too much material to cover in the normal in-service sessions used by the school district. With this in mind, Ms. Mitchell asked the teachers what they thought was the most important thing a classroom teacher needed to do a better job with at-risk students.

Juan Sanchez, a middle school math teacher, said, "We do not always know the problems that a student faces. We see them in class but don't know what their lives are like at home. Sometimes we don't see the problems until it's too late."

Wanda Stratton agreed that knowing which kids were at risk was a real problem. Ruth Jackson said, "It's true that you don't always know the problems that students have, but even when you do it doesn't help that much sometimes."

"What do you mean?" asked Mitchell.

"Well, say that you know a student isn't doing homework. You talk to the student and he tells you he works after school, gets home late, and falls asleep before he can finish his homework. You tell him to quit the job, but he says his family needs the money. I don't know what to do at that point. I'm not a social worker," lamented Ruth.

"Yeah, I have similar problems with some of the girls in my classes," said Wanda. "I can see them getting too serious about their boyfriends. I know they are likely to get pregnant, but what can I say or do?"

"OK, I think we may be getting somewhere," said Jo Mitchell. "First, classroom teachers need a better way—a more systematic way—of identifying who's at risk. This would include identifying the factors that put a student at risk. Second, classroom teachers need to learn tactics for dealing with the specific problems that put students at risk. If we were successful in dealing with these two things, I believe we would have a meaningful staff development program for the year."

After a few more minutes of discussion the teachers and principals agreed that the at-risk staff development program for the year should deal with showing teachers how to identify at-risk students and how to respond appropriately to the problems causing the risk.

Jo Mitchell contacted the School of Education at the local state university to seek advice from Larry Herbert, a professor who was well known for his research dealing with at-risk students. Ms. Mitchell made arrangements for him to meet with the group of principals and teachers who were helping her design the staff development program for the year. After discussing the staff development objectives with the committee, Professor Herbert offered to submit a proposal to the school district for a series of staff development workshops designed to improve the ability of classroom teachers to identify at-risk students and respond to their needs. Herbert stressed that the objectives of the committee could not be met with a single one-day workshop.

Two weeks later, Professor Herbert met with the committee to present a 12-page proposal that called for four 1-day workshops to be held over an 8-week period. Herbert's proposal made a distinction between cognitive learning and behavioral skills. He argued that most staff development efforts emphasize cognitive learning and downplay behavioral skills. The workshops designed by Herbert attempted to link cognitive and behavioral issues.

At the broadest level, the objectives for the workshop were (a) to train teachers to identify factors that put particular students at risk for academic failure and (b) to teach workshop participants to use specific tactics to reduce the impact of risk factors on particular students. All of the proposed workshops alternated between content-rich lectures and hands-on exercises aimed at increasing the practical skills of teachers in dealing with at-risk students. The design of the workshops is presented below.

Workshop I:
    This program was devoted to helping participants understand the factors that put students at risk for academic failure. This workshop relied heavily on an instrument developed by Professor Herbert called "The At-Risk Checklist." This checklist provided a simple, easy-to-use device for identifying the particular problems of each student.

Workshop II:
    This program was devoted to hands-on use of "The At-Risk Checklist." This workshop featured a series of case studies and critical incidents designed to give teachers the practice necessary to use the checklist accurately.

Workshop III:
    The third workshop was designed to familiarize teachers with specific tactics for responding to the problems of at-risk students. This workshop used a workbook called *Tactics for At-Risk Students: A Classroom Teacher's Guide.* The tactics in this workbook were keyed to the problems identified in the "At-Risk Checklist." This workshop focused on identifying the tactics appropriate to the specific factors that put a student at risk.

Workshop IV:
    The fourth workshop was designed to give participants practice in using the information and skills presented in the first three workshops. In addition to case studies, this workshop used a variety of role-playing exercises to give participants the experiential understanding necessary for mastery.

Professor Herbert's presentation lasted about 20 minutes and was followed by another 15 minutes of questions and discussion. At that point, Jo Mitchell thanked Professor Herbert for his presentation and indicated that he could leave the meeting. With another 10 minutes of discussion, the committee decided to accept Professor Herbert's proposal. The next morning Ms. Mitchell telephoned Professor Herbert and told him the committee had decided to accept his proposal.

Evaluation Issues

Focusing the Evaluation

Ms. Mitchell opened the meeting with the following questions: "How do we want to evaluate the at-risk staff development program? What data do we need to collect? How shall we interpret the data?"

Juan Sanchez said, "Let's compare the drop-out rate of the students in the district before and after the program."

"I doubt that you will see a difference in the drop-out rate immediately," said Mitchell. "That would be expecting too much too soon from a single staff development program. Our program will provide the teachers with a few more skills and some comfort in using those skills, but what we are doing here won't have an immediate, dramatic impact on the drop-out rate."

"Then why bother?" asked Tanya Greene.

"You bother because the program will have an impact on some of the teachers and some of the students they teach," answered Herbert.

"If the drop-out rate is not the right thing to measure, what is?" asked Sanchez.

"You can ask the teachers about the quality of the program," said Jo Mitchell. "You know, questions such as: 'Was the content of the workshop relevant to problems you face in the classroom? Did the trainer know the material? How skillfully did the trainer present the material? Will you be able to apply the lessons of the staff development workshop to your classroom? How satisfied were you with the workshop?' "

"I would rather do a workshop that had a real impact on the drop-out rate," replied Sanchez.

"I would, too," answered Mitchell. "But we don't have the funding to undertake a project massive enough to have a dramatic impact on the drop-out rate."

"So we are stuck with asking the teachers if they had a good time," Sanchez retorted.

"There's a wide range of effectiveness between 'we had a good time' and 'we cut the drop-out rate in half,' " Professor Herbert said. "The staff development program can be useful even if it doesn't cause a drastic change in a summary statistic such as the drop-out rate."

"I think Professor Herbert may have a point," said Tanya Greene. "Teachers can tell when a program will help them do a better job in the classroom. They are also sharp enough to know that they aren't going to learn enough in any one, two, three, or four workshops to keep the kids with the most serious problems from dropping out of school. So let's figure out how we can tell if these workshops are worth having."

"We should also keep in mind that the main reason for doing an evaluation is to help us improve staff development programs from year to year. Frequently, we are able to get information from an evaluation that helps us improve a staff development program before it is complete," said Jo Mitchell. With a few minutes of conversation, the committee agreed to develop a questionnaire that would evaluate each of the four workshops. They agreed that the questionnaire should evaluate the content of the workshops, presentation of the material, and the relevance of the techniques taught.

Developing Questionnaires

Using Standards and Indicators of Quality

Jo Mitchell took responsibility for developing the questionnaire and tabulating the results. As a first step in the development of the questionnaire, the committee examined the standards and indicators located in Resource A of this guide for help in focusing the evaluation. Because they had decided to concentrate on the teachers' opinions of the quality and usefulness of the workshops, the committee decided to use Standard 7 as a guide in developing evaluation instruments.

> **Standard 7:** *Staff Development Trainers.* The staff development trainers should be highly competent and have the backgrounds and experiences necessary to give them high credibility with participants.

The committee decided to design the questionnaire based on several of the indicators of quality listed for Standard 7. The selected indicators were:

7.1. The trainer should have special expertise in the program content.
7.2. The trainer's background and experience should be similar to the participants', or the trainer should have a well-recognized expertise that lends credibility to his or her efforts.
7.3. The staff development trainer should have the ability to develop rapport with participants and to demonstrate an understanding of the problems, priorities, and needs of participants.
7.4. Trainers should have a demonstrated knowledge of adult learning theory.
7.5. Trainers should be able to incorporate modeling, feedback, and coaching into their instructional strategies.

After reviewing the indicators, Jo Mitchell asked each member of the committee to submit several questions that might be included on the questionnaire. Within a week, committee members had sent her 47 potential questions. Mitchell found that 12 of the questions were essentially duplicates and several were too vague to determine the writer's intent. Most of the questions seemed pertinent, however, and she used them to construct a tentative questionnaire.

Using the General Guide

Because she was not an expert in questionnaire design, Mitchell consulted James Sanders's *Evaluating School Programs: An Educator's Guide* for advice about designing a questionnaire. She found the following guidelines:

- Provide clear instructions, including a due date.
- Don't ask leading questions.
- Group questions according to topic.
- Make it attractive.
- Do not assume too much knowledge.
- Begin by asking easy, impersonal questions.
- Don't ask double questions (i.e., two questions in one).
- State questions precisely.

She also went to the library and checked out two other books on questionnaires and survey research recommended by Sanders.

Mitchell began assembling her questionnaire by deciding on the categories or groups relevant to the suggested questions. Her categories were:

Program Content
Effectiveness of the Trainer
Usefulness of the Techniques

Next, Ms. Mitchell sorted her questions by category. She found that she had a large number of questions related to "Content of Workshop" and only two related to the "Usefulness of the Techniques." She also had four questions that did not seem to fit in to any of the three categories. Studying the four questions, Mitchell decided on a fourth category: "Workshop Format." Looking at the distribution of questions, she knew that she would have to eliminate some questions from the first category and create additional questions for the last two categories.

Some of the suggested questions were too vague to be used. She discarded the following questions on the basis of vagueness:

- Was it a good program all around?
- Did you enjoy the program?

Several of the suggested items were double statements. The two themes represented in double statements were revised as two separate items. Two examples of this problem and Jo Mitchell's solutions are presented in Table 4.1. The final version of the Workshop Evaluation Questionnaire is shown in Table 4.2.

TABLE 4.1 Examples of Revised Double Statements

Double Statement
- The content of the program applies to my classroom and the instructor was well prepared for the session.

Revised as:
- The topics covered in this program apply directly to the problems of my students.
- The workshop instructor was well prepared for the session.

Double Statement
- The facilities were good and the length of the program was about right.

Revised as:
- The classroom was well suited to this type of program.
- Given the objectives of today's program, the length of the program was appropriate.

Collecting Data

To keep the size of the workshops manageable, Jo Mitchell decided to schedule two sections of each of the four workshops. Professor Herbert taught one section of each of the four workshops, and Larry Pettrie, another professor from the university, taught the remaining workshops. Pettrie was a young assistant professor in Herbert's department with a reputation as a demanding teacher and promising researcher.

The first workshops were scheduled on a regular staff development day, on the Monday 2 weeks prior to the opening of the fall semester. The workshops ran from 9:00 a.m. to 4:00 p.m., with an hour for lunch and two 15-minute breaks. At about 10 minutes to 4, the staff development coordinator, Jo Mitchell, distributed the workshop evaluation questionnaires to the participants in each of the sections. As she distributed the questionnaires, she read the following instructions:

Using Systematic Procedures

"Please complete this evaluation of today's workshop. Your responses to this questionnaire are important for helping us to understand how useful this program is. Your responses will also help us to improve future workshops. Answer each of the questions honestly, and be sure to write something in the comments section, as the comments provide some of the most helpful feedback on a workshop."

text continued on p. 66

TABLE 4.2 Workshop Evaluation Questionnaire

Name of the workshop:_____   Instructor:_____

INSTRUCTIONS: For each of the items below, please circle the response that most closely describes your evaluation of this workshop. You are also encouraged to provide written comments concerning the effectiveness of the workshop and the instructor. Your responses to these questions and any comments you write will be treated as confidential. Your candidness is appreciated. Do not put your name on this questionnaire.

PROGRAM CONTENT

1. Program objectives were clearly presented at the beginning of the workshop.

   Strongly Agree   Agree   Neutral   Disagree   Strongly Disagree

2. The topics presented were clearly related to the objectives of the workshop.

   Strongly Agree   Agree   Neutral   Disagree   Strongly Disagree

3. The amount of time given to each topic was appropriate.

   Strongly Agree   Agree   Neutral   Disagree   Strongly Disagree

4. The level of the program was appropriate to my background.

   Strongly Agree   Agree   Neutral   Disagree   Strongly Disagree

EFFECTIVENESS OF THE INSTRUCTOR

5. The instructor was knowledgeable about the program content.

   Strongly Agree   Agree   Neutral   Disagree   Strongly Disagree

6. The instructor was well prepared.

   Strongly Agree   Agree   Neutral   Disagree   Strongly Disagree

7. The instructor encouraged group participation.

   Strongly Agree   Agree   Neutral   Disagree   Strongly Disagree

8. The instructor made material accessible to workshop participants.

   Strongly Agree   Agree   Neutral   Disagree   Strongly Disagree

USEFULNESS OF TECHNIQUES

9. The material presented in this workshop was theoretically sound.

   Strongly Agree   Agree   Neutral   Disagree   Strongly Disagree

10. This workshop will make me a better teacher.

    Strongly Agree   Agree   Neutral   Disagree   Strongly Disagree

11. This material was extremely practical.

    Strongly Agree   Agree   Neutral   Disagree   Strongly Disagree

TABLE 4.2 Continued

12. This workshop allowed me to gain practical mastery of the skills taught.

    Strongly Agree   Agree   Neutral   Disagree   Strongly Disagree

WORKSHOP FORMAT

13. There was an appropriate amount of lecture in this workshop.

    Strongly Agree   Agree   Neutral   Disagree   Strongly Disagree

14. There was an appropriate amount of discussion in this workshop.

    Strongly Agree   Agree   Neutral   Disagree   Strongly Disagree

15. The instructor did a good job of modeling the skills taught.

    Strongly Agree   Agree   Neutral   Disagree   Strongly Disagree

16. The workshop provided adequate opportunity to practice the skills taught.

    Strongly Agree   Agree   Neutral   Disagree   Strongly Disagree

Comments on the Workshop

_____

_____

_____

_____

_____

_____

_____

_____

_____

_____

_____

TABLE 4.3 Data Analysis Summary Sheet: At-Risk Workshop Series

Workshop: *Workshop I*

INSTRUCTOR	*HERBERT*	*PETTRIE*
Program Content		
1. Clear objectives	4.5	4.1
2. Topics related to objectives	4.0	3.1
3. Appropriate time given each topic	4.4	3.4
4. Appropriate level of content	4.3	2.6
Effectiveness of Instructor		
5. Instructor knowledge	4.6	4.4
6. Instructor preparation	4.3	4.3
7. Level of participation	4.4	2.8
8. Materials are accessible	4.6	2.4
Usefulness of Techniques		
9. Theoretically sound	4.4	4.2
10. Become a better teacher	4.2	2.8
11. Extremely practical	4.5	2.8
12. Practical mastery	4.1	2.3
Workshop Format		
13. Appropriate amount of lecture	4.0	2.2
14. Appropriate amount of discussion	4.2	2.1
15. Instructor modeled skills	3.9	1.9
16. Appropriate practice of skills	4.1	1.9

NOTE: Strongly Disagree = 1; Strongly Agree = 5.

"Please do not put your name on the questionnaires. I would like one of you to collect the completed questionnaires, seal them in this envelope, and return them to me this afternoon. As these instructions suggest, your responses are confidential. Thank you for your cooperation."

Analyzing and Interpreting Data

The next day, Jo Mitchell and two of the teachers on the staff development committee tabulated the responses to the questionnaires and calculated the average score for each item. The tabulation sheet appears in Table 4.3.

As data in the table show, the workshop conducted by Professor Herbert was rated highly on all items. Only one person rated any of the items as low as a 3 on the 5-point scale. The comments on the questionnaires from Professor Herbert's workshop were consistent with the high ratings on the quantitative items.

The workshop conducted by Professor Pettrie received much lower ratings on a number of items. Although participants in Pettrie's workshop rated the content of the session rather highly, the ratings for presentation style were considerably less positive. The following statements taken from the Comments section of the questionnaire for Pettrie's workshop are representative of the participants' concerns:

"Too dry and boring."

"The presentation was too theoretical."

"Pedantic."

"Too much emphasis given to the research literature."

"Not practical."

"I was bored out of my gourd. We never got a chance to ask questions or discuss anything."

"Don't talk down to me. I'm a professional with a master's degree and 15 years of experience."

Applying the Findings

Jo Mitchell telephoned Professor Pettrie and asked him to meet with her. Mitchell opened the meeting with Pettrie by telling him that she had reviewed the evaluation questionnaire for his workshop and was concerned about some aspects of the response. Handing Pettrie the summary sheet and the comments from teachers, Mitchell said, "Larry, I would like you to take a look at the ratings and the comments from the questionnaire."

Constructive Confrontation

Pettrie took the summary page and the typed comments. He studied them intently, spending almost 5 minutes reading and re-reading them. Finally, he said, "Wow. I'm surprised. I had no idea they felt this way. They really hated me."

"That's much too harsh. They don't hate you. They just responded negatively to some aspects of your presentation style."

"But I don't understand how this happened. I taught the way I always teach, and I never get this kind of reaction."

"Well, who do you usually teach?" asked Mitchell.

"My students at the university."

"And how old are they?" asked Mitchell.

"They're 20-21 for the most part. Sophomores and juniors," answered Pettrie.

"And how much teaching experience do they have?"

"Generally, none," answered Pettrie.

"I think that may be most of the problem with the workshop," said Mitchell. "Most of our teachers are 10-20-30 years older than your students at the university. Most of them have many years of classroom experience."

"That's why I made an extra effort to be well prepared. I made sure I had all the *i*s dotted and *t*s crossed on the research literature. I didn't want an experienced teacher tripping me up," responded Pettrie.

At this point Professor Herbert said, "You were worried about the wrong thing. Experienced teachers are not going to question your expertise as a scholar or researcher. They are more concerned with whether or not you understand the practical problems they face in the classroom every day. They want to know if you have practical advice for handling their practical problems. I guess I should have briefed you better when I asked you to do the workshop."

"Okay. I can modify my approach to put more emphasis on practical problems. What else?" asked Pettrie.

"Well, both the comments and the quantitative responses suggest that you need to let the teachers participate more. You need to let them ask questions. You need to let them respond to each other and learn from each other. You should ask questions at key points, and generally encourage dialogue," said Mitchell.

They concluded the session with a detailed discussion about Pettrie's plans for the next workshop. When it was time for the second workshop, Herbert and Pettrie switched groups. The same questionnaire was administered at the end of the second workshop. Professor Pettrie's ratings increased substantially, with most of the items rated either 4 or 5. The presentation style scores increased dramatically. The written comments were consistent with the quantitative scores. Professor Herbert's scores for the second workshop were consistent with those from his first workshop. Using the same questionnaire and the same procedures, both Pettrie and Herbert received high ratings for the third and fourth workshops.

Summary of Evaluation Principles

1. There was vigorous debate among most stakeholders during the period in which the workshops were designed and the evaluation was focused. There was a good discussion of what variables ought to be measured and how they should be measured.

2. This particular evaluation project used an outside consultant with special expertise regarding the education of at-risk students. The consultant was brought into the evaluation discussion early on and his advice was followed in some detail.

3. The questionnaire used to evaluate the workshops was very carefully designed. The person developing the questionnaire was guided by the standards and indicators of quality in Resource A of this guide, solicited potential questions from a number of people in-

volved in the workshop, and was very careful in crafting the items used on the questionnaire.

4. The questionnaire was administered systematically, confidentiality of responses was maintained, the data were systematically analyzed, and the results carefully interpreted.

5. The evaluation was formative or developmental in nature. When one of the workshop instructors developed problems in communicating with participants, the results of the evaluation were used to help the instructor improve his approach.

Alternative Strategies

Other Approaches The questionnaire used in this evaluation collected data from teachers. School principals, counselors, and other members of the professional staff may have been good sources of information concerning teachers' use of effective approaches for dealing with at-risk students. When they focused the evaluation, the team rejected proposals to measure outcomes such as the drop-out rate. Including parents and at-risk students, however, may have been useful for collecting outcome data regarding tactics taught in the workshops.

Cautions Regarding Misinterpretation

The evaluation was based on the administration of a self-designed questionnaire. Although the questionnaire was carefully designed, it was administered to a small group of teachers. This type of questionnaire may do an adequate job of measuring how satisfied participants were with the workshops. We have no information at all, however, about the impact of these workshops on the success of at-risk students.

5 Vignette Five

Enhancing Multicultural Perspectives in a Private School

Background **P**ortola Canyon School is a highly selective private school located in an exclusive residential suburb of a major West Coast city. Even though the school's tuition is more than $8,000 per year, few families request or need financial aid. The Porsches, Corvettes, Mercedes, and BMWs peppering the student parking lot reflect the affluence of students attending the school. Although the surrounding communities have large Hispanic, African-American, and Asian populations, more than 90% of the students at Portola Canyon School are white.

The headmaster, some of the teachers, and two key members of the Board of Trustees were uncomfortable with the situation. According to the headmaster, Jay Livingston, "We look like a white enclave in the midst of a sea of diversity, and I believe that does a disservice to our youngsters. They are going to live in a multicultural world, and we should prepare them for that world."

Livingston's views were not universally shared. The comments of some parents made it clear that they valued Portola largely because it did *not* reflect the wider community. Similarly, some of the teachers cherished the elite nature of the school and valued the opportunity to work with students from "the right families." When Livingston began to discuss the need for honoring diversity and building a multicultural perspective into the curriculum, he discovered that there was a core of about eight faculty members who actively spoke against the concept.

Nonetheless, Livingston decided to initiate a Multicultural Appreciation Program the following school year. To organize the new program, he appointed a Multicultural Appreciation Task Force consisting of six teachers, four students, and two administrators. Five of the six teachers ranged from lukewarm to enthusiastic in their views on promoting diversity and multiculturalism. The sixth teacher saw "many pitfalls with this concept." Of the four students, one was African American, one was Hispanic, one was Asian, and one was white. The two administrators on the committee were the headmaster and the director of student life. This committee met several times during the spring semester to set goals and make plans for the next school year.

Planning a Workshop

Aware of the controversy surrounding his decision to promote diversity and multiculturalism, Livingston knew that the staff development workshop used to kick off the Multicultural Appreciation Program would need to be carefully planned, skillfully executed, and thoroughly evaluated. Livingston wanted a workshop that would both increase awareness and change the behavior of members of the school community regarding issues of diversity and multiculturalism.

Mr. Livingston appointed Jean Taylor, one of the teachers on the task force, to coordinate the evaluation. He selected her because she was a systematic, organized person with a reputation for getting things done on time. She was also recognized among the teachers as a fair-minded person with no particular ax to grind.

Mr. Livingston told her that she could use the secretarial resources and supplies of the headmaster's office to conduct the evaluation. He indicated that he would like a preliminary evaluation early in the fall and a more comprehensive evaluation by the end of the spring semester. He also indicated that he expected the members of the task force to assist her in planning and conducting the evaluation. The task force first discussed evaluation during the third planning meeting in the spring. To get the discussion started, Taylor asked, "How will we be able to tell if the efforts to promote a multicultural perspective at Portola Canyon School have been successful?"

Members of the committee offered a variety of answers. One teacher argued, "The program is successful if the teachers respond positively to it." Someone else added, "It's a success if teachers change their behavior." One of the students on the committee said, "Ask the students if they notice a difference." Another student said, "The students will change their attitudes and behavior."

Focusing the Evaluation

"It's doubtful that we can measure all of these things. Which one is the most important?" asked Taylor.

"The attitudes and behavior of the students is the most important factor," insisted Ruth Lowenthal, a senior English teacher. "After all," she continued, "it doesn't matter how much we congratulate ourselves on what a wonderful job we are doing if nothing really changes for the students."

After considerable discussion, the task force agreed that it was probably more important to focus on the students than on any other group.

"Can we measure the impact of a particular staff development program on the students?" asked Taylor. "Isn't that a bit much to expect from a single workshop?"

"Perhaps, but I think we are just wasting our time if we can't see any difference at the student level. We ought to have the courage to see if our staff development works or if it is just a waste of time," retorted Lowenthal.

"Okay, let's follow Ruth's logic and see what it means in terms of evaluation," said Taylor. "Are we interested in both attitudes and behavior, or just behavior?" she asked.

"Both," responded several people simultaneously.

Using Standards and Indicators of Quality

At that point, Taylor asked the committee members to examine the standards and indicators in Resource A of this guide. After reviewing the standards, they decided that the follow-up and reinforcement stressed by the two indicators for Standard 9 were pertinent to this situation:

9.1. There should be systematic procedures for determining the extent to which skills and cognitive materials are applied on the job.

9.2. There should be follow-up activities to reinforce program learning.

In the context of Standard 9, the committee began to look at its options for measuring both attitudes and behavior. The members of the committee considered the strengths and weaknesses of attitude surveys, interviews, behavior observation scales, and focus groups. The committee agreed that a focus group would be the most appropriate. They favored the focus group because it was very personal and could deal with complex, subtle, and sensitive issues. Although they were aware that results from focus group studies often do not generalize to larger groups, they thought this limitation could be overcome by the fact that most of the small number of minority students in the district would be included in the focus groups.

The Multicultural Appreciation Project Workshop

The staff development workshop was held in mid-August and included teachers, administrators, counselors, and student life personnel as participants. The workshop opened with a panel discussion by the four students who had been on the planning task force the previous spring. For the first hour of the session, the students talked about how difficult it was to be a member of a school community in which they were very different from most of the other students. They spoke of often feeling lonely, isolated, invisible, and alienated. In some cases the teachers seemed to ignore their presence, seldom calling on them even when they raised their hands. Yet, in other circumstances they felt highly visible and vulnerable. Some teachers seemed to single them out, treating them as experts or representatives for an entire race, ethnic group, or neighborhood.

The white student on the panel stressed how much she had learned working with the other students on the task force. She said that she was unaware of the cliquishness of the campus until she had an opportunity to see Portola Canyon School through the eyes of minority students.

After the panel discussion, which lasted about an hour, the workshop coordinator called a break. Following the break, the participants alternated between small-group meetings and reporting the results of those meetings to the entire group. The job of the small groups was to suggest ways for the school to become more inviting and inclusive for students and faculty of diverse, multicultural backgrounds. As the proposed changes were announced by the small groups, a comprehensive list was made on newsprint and posted around the large meeting room.

By the 2:30 p.m. break, several dozen suggestions were posted around the room. The first task for the 3:00 p.m.–5:00 p.m. session was to discuss the merits of the suggestions and narrow the list to the 20 ideas that could be implemented easily and inexpensively. The second task was to obtain a commitment from everyone in the room to implement changes.

Dealing With Conflict

As soon as the purpose of the last segment of the workshop was explained, several of the teachers began raising concerns about the appropriateness of changing courses and activities so close to the opening of school. They pointed out that they had spent a good part of the summer preparing for the upcoming school year and insisted that it was unfair to ask them to make changes now, no matter how worthy the goal. Two other teachers insisted that they did not have enough time to cover all of the material that needed to be covered in the first place. They argued that they could not possibly find room for additional material in their courses, no matter when they were notified.

When a complete impasse appeared likely, Headmaster Livingston stated that the proposed changes would not be mandatory. He also pointed out that it was unlikely that any teacher would be able to implement more than a few of the proposed changes. He asked if they could agree to go forward on that basis. At this point one teacher called the whole workshop "a waste of time" and characterized multiculturalism as "just one more hare-brained scheme destined to go the way of every other useless educational fad of the last 30 years." The rest of the workshop participants, however, agreed to select 20 ideas that seemed worthy of implementing. It took about 45 minutes to agree on the list of 20 changes that would help incorporate a multicultural perspective into the school's curriculum, programs, and activities.

Livingston considered the commitment that the faculty made to change was a major success. He took every opportunity to reinforce the school's commitment to multiculturalism. At each monthly faculty meeting, Mr. Livingston had at least two different faculty members report on their own progress toward meeting the goal of making the campus community more aware of multicultural issues. He encouraged questions and comments about the Multicultural Appreciation Program and teachers enthusiastically shared ideas in this setting.

Strategy for Collecting Information

Focus Groups

The Multicultural Appreciation Program was evaluated using focus groups. A focus group is a qualitative research method used to explore complex and subtle issues in depth. These groups generally contain 6 to 12 people who are similar to each other in important ways. A focus group is useful for exploring the opinions of a small subgroup of people. The similarity of the people in the group helps them to feel comfortable revealing their opinions on issues. Another characteristic of focus groups is their concentration on a small number of topics or issues. It is the job of the focus group leader to promote openness and stimulate discussion.

There were three separate focus groups. One focus group was for minority students, one was for nonminority students, and one was for teachers. All three of the focus groups were facilitated by Dr. Jane Miller, a counselor at the school with experience conducting focus groups.

Selecting Focus Group Participants

Each focus group contained 10 members. The participants in each focus group were selected because of their similarities to members of the groups they represented. The minority students' focus group contained five African American students, three Hispanic students, and two Asian students. Participants were selected randomly from the minority students at Portola Canyon School. The participants in the focus group for nonminority students were selected randomly from the school's nonminority students. After eliminating teachers known to be either enthusiastically for or antagonistically against the Multicultural Appreciation Program, Mrs. Taylor randomly selected 10 teachers to participate in a focus group session. This composition of the teachers' group was designed to allow the voice of the majority of the teachers, rather than those on the extremes of the issue, to be heard.

The focus group for minority students was conducted first. The session lasted about an hour and a half, was fast-paced, enthusiastic, friendly, and sometimes tense. The facilitator introduced herself to the group and asked each participant to introduce himself or herself. Dr. Miller explained that Portola Canyon School had asked her to help the school understand how well the Multicultural Appreciation Program was working and what might be done to improve it. As part of the ground rules, Dr. Miller explained that the information shared in the focus group was confidential. She went on to say that confidentiality meant that they were not to discuss this information after leaving the group and that none of the things said in the group would be publicly attributed to anyone in the group. The group coordinator asked permission to use a tape recorder in each of the groups, promising to erase the tape after making notes of the meeting.

With a quick laugh she asked, "Okay, has anybody here heard of this thing, this Multicultural Appreciation Program?" The students laughed and smiled.

"Sure," answered Harold. "Mr. Livingston is always saying something about it in assembly. It seems to be a big deal to him."

Dr. Miller asked if anyone else had heard of the program. Nine of the 10 students had. In addition to Mr. Livingston, a variety of teachers, coaches, and counselors had discussed the program at some length in classes, assemblies, and other settings.

Dr. Miller then asked a variety of open-ended questions, listening carefully and nondefensively to whatever answers the students provided. Typical of the questions asked were:

"How well do you think the Multicultural Appreciation Program is working at the moment?"

"Could you point to some specific things that worked particularly well? What's not working at the moment?"

The focus group coordinator did a good job of asking open-ended questions, of avoiding leading questions, and of asking questions that probed people's feelings or elicited greater information—questions such as, "Did any of your teachers discuss the contributions to their academic field made by different cultures?" "If so, how did you feel when this information was presented?" "Can you say more about that?" "Then what happened?" "Does anyone have a different view or impression of that?"

Using similar techniques, Dr. Miller conducted the focus group sessions for the other two groups. In the teachers' focus group, only 8 of the 10 selected teachers attended the focus group. The 2 who did not attend telephoned Jean Taylor to apologize and explain their reasons for being unable to attend. Taylor regarded the excuses as credible. All of the students selected for the nonminority student focus group attended.

Focus Group Results

The minority students in their focus group reported few real changes in the behavior or attitudes of their fellow students. They did point out, however, that there was a lot more talk about other cultures and ethnic groups in their classes and on campus. They had noticed that teachers had given more attention to things like Black History Month and the birthday of Martin Luther King, Jr. The students pointed out that there was going to be a school-wide celebration of Cinco de Mayo in a few weeks.

Some of the students spoke of the heightened pride they felt when a teacher took time to present and discuss issues related directly to their heritage. Some thought that a few of "the special teachers" were extremely enthusiastic about the Multicultural Appreciation Program and had done a wonderful job in bringing broader, more inclusive perspectives to their classrooms. These teachers, they said, made everyone feel special. Three of the students said specifically that they felt much more welcome and included in the life of the campus this year. The United Nations Day held in November and the International Festival held in March were singled out as positive events that tended to make people look at the world less narrowly.

There were a number of complaints, however. Some of the teachers paid no attention at all to diversity issues and had not changed any of their attitudes or behaviors with regard to minority students. Those teachers were referred to as "hard cases" and "cold dudes." Other teachers were credited with making an effort but were seen as awkward and uncomfortable trying to do so.

The focus group for nonminority students was calmer than those of either the minority students or the teachers. All of the students in the group were aware of the Multicultural Appreciation Program and 6 of the 10 explicitly endorsed the program as worthwhile. One student commented that the program was good because most Portola students need to be reminded of how privileged they were. Two had worked as tutors for students in an inner-city school, and both spoke about how startled they were at the poverty and how satisfying it was to be helpful.

The teachers' focus group came to the following conclusions: That it was difficult to bring a multicultural perspective to many of the subjects; that math and science are difficult to present from a multicultural perspective; that most of the textbooks do not have material that makes it easy to do, so that it is necessary to find materials on your own and that that is very time consuming. When successful in bringing a multicultural perspective to a course, there is heightened interest and motivation among all students, minority and nonminority alike. When it works, the class discussions are among the most stimulating of the semester. There were several comments to the effect that, "I'm lost; this is hard; I don't know how to do this." There were others who said, "I had good intentions but I felt awkward and clumsy doing this." Several of the teachers suggested that, "If we're going to do this, let's do it right. We need more resources, perhaps different textbooks, and additional workshops to help us learn to do this well."

Interpretation of the Results

Standard 9 stressed the importance of follow-up to make certain that gains made as a result of training are reinforced and maintained. The student focus groups were designed to assess the impact of the multicultural workshops at the student level. The teacher focus group was designed to determine where there were problems implementing the program launched by the workshop.

The students recognized that many teachers had implemented changes aimed at bringing a multicultural perspective to their classrooms. The focus group leader reported that the workshop seemed to have had uneven results across the curriculum. The students and teachers both recognized that it was more difficult to bring a multicultural perspective to math and science courses.

Both students and teachers indicated that Mr. Livingston was a big supporter of multiculturalism. The teachers noted that little would have happened without his continuing follow-up and support of the staff development workshop. The teachers were more perceptive than students in recognizing problems with changing the curriculum. They were aware of how difficult the task was and how few resources were available to bring a multicultural perspective into the classroom. Specifically, the teachers asked for more teaching resources and additional staff development workshops concentrated on multicultural issues.

Applying the Evaluation Results

Responding to Findings

Over the summer, the school purchased about $2,000 worth of additional materials and set up a Multicultural Appreciation Resource Center in the library. These resources included videotapes on the history of Africa and Asia. There was also a video on Hispanic influences in the Americas. The school also purchased a set of syllabi based on a model curriculum noted for its multicultural perspective. The most useful aspect of the model curriculum was a set of handouts that were keyed to the syllabi. Teachers were able to photocopy the handouts for use in their classrooms or for the preparation of lectures or activities. A staff development workshop with the theme of "Integrating Multicultural Perspectives Into the Curriculum" was planned for the following August.

Summary of Evaluation Principles

1. Evaluation was part of the planning process for the initial staff development workshop.
2. A trained and experienced focus group leader was used to conduct focus group sessions.
3. Data were collected systematically and analyzed objectively.
4. The focus group leader skillfully used open-ended questions to elicit subtle and complex information. Focus groups also proved to be a good way to elicit criticisms or negative information.
5. The confidentiality of all participants in the focus groups was protected. Assurances of confidentiality encourage participants to voice criticisms or share negative information.
6. An emphasis on problem solving and program improvement, and not on the evaluation of individuals, reduced the incentive for people to distort the information or give socially desirable answers.
7. The information was systematically collected, organized, analyzed, and fed back to the school.
8. Evaluation information resulted in changes in the Multicultural Appreciation Program.

Alternate Strategies for Evaluation

Other Approaches

There are several additional ways in which information about the Multicultural Appreciation Program could have been collected. If the task force had decided to concentrate on attitude change, an attitude survey could have been administered. In this approach to data collection, an attitude survey could have been administered to students and/or teachers to determine the extent to which their attitudes favored valuing diversity and multiculturalism. The attitude survey could then have been administered to students and teachers at the end of the spring semester, and it would have been possible to compare changes in attitude. The disadvantages of this approach are that an attitude scale would have had to been developed or a commercially available form would have had to been located. Both of these are usually difficult and time-consuming processes. Knowing the extent to which attitudes have or have not changed may not be particularly helpful in providing formative guidance for a multicultural appreciation program. Attitude surveys do not tell you how to go about changing things.

Another approach to evaluating the staff development workshop would have been a very simple one of asking the participants in the workshop to fill out a questionnaire that indicated the extent to which they were satisfied with the workshop. The major advantages of this approach are speed and low cost. The disadvantage of this approach is that it does not tell you the extent to which the workshop had an impact on what the teachers do in their classrooms or whether or not students are impacted at all.

A third alternate strategy to data collection would have been to conduct interviews with teachers and students to see to what extent the Multicultural Appreciation Program had been effective in the school. Interviews require the development of an interview protocol that lists the specific questions to be asked. The interviewer needs to ask all participants roughly the same questions in roughly the same order. Interviews are quite time consuming and the results are sometimes difficult to interpret.

Cautions Regarding Misinterpretation

A focus group is a subjective way to collect data. The quality of the information depends on the skill of the focus group coordinator, the quality of the questions asked, and the insight of the focus group participants. If the focus group participants are not representative of the group from which they were selected, generalizations will be faulty. The personal, face-to-face nature of a focus group may encourage some respondents to give socially desirable answers to sensitive questions. The study would have been strengthened by using multiple sources of information.

6

Vignette Six

Evaluating Self-Esteem Workshops

Background Stevens Elementary School, located in the town of Stevens Park, Illinois, was part of a small suburban school district. The district's staff development coordinator, Helen Hensen, worked with the teachers and the principal of Stevens Elementary School to develop the annual staff development workshop schedule and plan. Janice Stayer was a woman in her early forties with 6 years of experience as principal of Stevens Elementary School. She had been a 4th-grade teacher in another school before becoming the principal of this K-6 school. Ms. Hensen taught half time as a junior high school science teacher and served as the district's staff development coordinator. In considering staff development priorities for the upcoming year, Stayer and Hensen noted that many of the students in the school district seemed to lack self-confidence and have low initiative. As they discussed this problem, they decided that it might be appropriate to have a staff development workshop that would help teachers do a better job of promoting the self-esteem of their students. Hensen and Stayer met with several teachers to discuss the usefulness of a workshop that would help teachers in this way. The teachers were very positive about including a self-esteem workshop as part of their regular in-service training.

As she began to make arrangements for a self-esteem workshop, Hensen decided to seek some advice from Professor Sam Schulman, a professor of psychology at the nearby state university. She had taken a course from Professor Schulman several years earlier and remembered that he conducted research on self-esteem. She contacted Schulman and asked him about the possibility of designing and coordinating such a workshop. Professor Schulman was eager to get involved and met with Hensen and Stayer a few days later to present a workshop proposal to them.

The workshop design was based on five principles for promoting self-esteem in elementary school students. The principles were:

1. Recognize the unique abilities and talents of each student.
2. Learn to understand the behavior of students in terms of their personalities and where they are developmentally.
3. Show acceptance of students and respect for their self-worth, whether or not they are demonstrating positive behavior.
4. Learn to use classroom strategies and techniques that promote a sense of competence, self-worth, and positive self-regard in students.
5. Learn to avoid classroom tactics that deflate, put down, criticize, or demean students.

The workshop was composed of three modules; each module contained four components. The four components of each module are listed below.

1. The first component of each module was a brief lecture—perhaps 10 or 15 minutes—on an aspect of self-esteem theory.
2. During the second module, participants would work in small groups, applying the principles of self-esteem to a case study.
3. The third component was a videotape demonstrating or modeling the appropriate esteem-building behavior for a particular situation.
4. The fourth component was a role-playing exercise designed to allow participants to practice the techniques modeled in the videotape.

The workshop taught teachers how to improve their students' self-esteem by recognizing their accomplishments, showing the students how to be comfortable in asking to have their needs met, encouraging students to express their true feelings, giving them positive and constructive ways to ventilate their feelings, and helping them feel good about themselves even when they faced failure or disappointment.

Planning for the Evaluation

Focusing the Evaluation
When Janice Stayer and Helen Hensen were satisfied with the design of the self-esteem workshops, they began to discuss program evaluation strategies with Professor Schulman. Helen Hensen sug-

gested that they use the standards and indicators in Resource A as a guide to focus their evaluation. They agreed that Standard 8 provided an appropriate focus for evaluating the workshop's effectiveness.

> **Standard 8:** *Meeting Course/Activity Objectives.* The school should have a mechanism for determining the extent to which the objectives for staff development courses and activities have been accomplished.

The most pertinent indicator for measuring this Standard was 8.2:

> 8.2. Follow-up activities should monitor the effectiveness of the application of program content to job activities.

Before settling on the final evaluation strategy to be used, Schulman, Stayer, and Hensen discussed and rejected two other approaches. The first approach employed a one-page evaluation form administered at the end of the session. This form would have asked how effectively the trainer had presented the material, how appropriate the material was to the goals of the workshop, and how satisfied the teachers were with the workshop. This is the most common approach to evaluating staff development workshops because it is straightforward, convenient, and inexpensive. It was rejected in this case because Stayer and Hensen wanted a more "results-oriented" evaluation. A second approach would have been to measure the self-esteem of students before and after the workshop. This approach was rejected because it is difficult for kindergarten, 1st-, and 2nd-grade students to complete the questionnaires normally used with older children who are able read and respond to a scale. Also, it is unrealistic to expect students to change their behavior immediately after teachers complete a workshop.

The third approach, the one adopted for the workshop, relied on observing teachers in their classrooms to determine how effectively they were applying the skills learned in the self-esteem workshop. Hensen, Stayer, and Schulman discussed the advantages of direct observation, the likely resistance of teachers to this approach, and related issues. Schulman suggested using his graduate students as in-class observers. Janice Stayer argued that having the graduate students in the classrooms as evaluators would make the teachers nervous, and she predicted considerable resistance from teachers on this point.

Involvement of Stakeholders   Because the teachers' responses were critical to the success of the program, Stayer proposed a meeting with teachers to discuss the workshop and the proposed evaluation strategy. During the subsequent meeting, the teachers were enthusiastic about the self-esteem workshop, but they were wary about the prospect of observers visiting their classrooms to evaluate them. Schulman stressed that the intention was to evaluate the effectiveness of the workshops, not the teachers. Ms. Hensen pointed out that the goal of evaluation is developmental; the focus is on program improvement.

One of the teachers suggested that using a camera to videotape classes might be less intrusive and distracting than having a stranger in the classroom. Someone else suggested that teachers would be more comfortable if only volunteers were involved in the evaluation. Schulman argued that this would bias the results, but he received little support from anyone else in the meeting. Near the end of the meeting, they agreed to use volunteers and to videotape classes of teachers who agreed to be part of the evaluation.

Strategy for Collecting Information

The data collection strategy called for teachers to be rated on their self-esteem-building skills before and after the workshop. This research design is called a pretest/posttest design. Janice Stayer sent a memo to her teachers explaining the workshop and asking for volunteers to participate in the evaluation. Eleven teachers contacted her to find out more details, but only 8 volunteered when they learned that they would have to have two classes videotaped—one before the workshop and another 6 weeks later. Arrangements were made to set up unattended cameras in the classrooms of the volunteers. At the end of the class, one of Professor Schulman's graduate students came in, turned off the camera, collected the videotape, labeled it with the teacher's name, and put away the equipment. A videotape was completed for each teacher who had volunteered to participate in the evaluation.

Schulman developed a data-collection form called the Self-Esteem Behavioral Observation Scale. The scale consisted of a large number of behaviors that a teacher might exhibit in class. The items on the scale were drawn from the theoretical and empirical literature on self-esteem. To rate a teacher's behavior, an observer made a check mark on the form beside the behavior observed. A value of +1 was assigned to each behavior that promoted self-esteem and a −1 was assigned to each behavior that diminished self-esteem. A total score for a teacher could be calculated by summing the checked items.

Professor Schulman trained the observers to use the Behavior Observation Scale by having them rate the behaviors observed on the training tapes used for the workshops. He worked with the observers in small groups, explaining how and why particular behaviors promote or diminish self-esteem. The observers were taught to detect

TABLE 6.1 Self-Esteem Study Summary Rating Sheet: Pretest Data

	Rater A Number of Observations		Rater B Number of Observations	
	Promoting Behaviors	*Diminishing Behaviors*	*Promoting Behaviors*	*Diminishing Behaviors*
Teacher 1	12	8	13	9
Teacher 2	7	8	7	8
Teacher 3	2	15	2	15
Teacher 4	9	7	10	7
Teacher 5	8	11	8	11
Teacher 6	14	5	14	6
Teacher 7	13	1	13	0
Teacher 8	2	22	2	22
Average	8.375	9.625	8.625	9.75

rather subtle behaviors as well as more obvious behaviors. The trainees practiced until they could consistently identify and classify the relevant behaviors.

Results of the Ratings of the Videotapes

Training Raters for Consistency

The researchers took about 2 weeks to complete the viewing and rating of the videotapes collected before the workshop. To increase the reliability of their ratings, each videotape was rated by two trained observers. The ratings of the videotaped performances of teachers are presented below. There is a high degree of consistency between ratings given by each observer. This degree of consistency indicates that the measuring procedures were, in one important sense, reliable.

The ratings of the pretest videotapes for the eight teachers are summarized in Table 6.1. Rater A and Rater B scored each teacher's videotape very consistently. The consistency (reliability) in ratings suggested that the data were sound. The results of the ratings were not shared with participants before the workshop.

Six weeks after the workshop, Professor Schulman's graduate students again arranged to videotape the classes of the eight volunteers. These videotapes were analyzed and rated in the same manner as the first set. Two different observers (Rater C and Rater D) rated the videotapes made after the workshop. The videotapes made before the workshop are called pretest tapes. The videotapes made after the workshop are called posttest tapes. The results of the analysis of the posttest tapes are presented in Table 6.2. As had been the case with the pretest data, the raters (C & D) for the posttest videotapes were

TABLE 6.2 Self-Esteem Study Summary Rating Sheet: Posttest Data

| | Rater C | | Rater D | |
| | Number of Observations | | Number of Observations | |
	Promoting Behaviors	Diminishing Behaviors	Promoting Behaviors	Diminishing Behaviors
Teacher 1	18	4	18	3
Teacher 2	12	5	12	5
Teacher 3	3	11	3	11
Teacher 4	16	5	18	5
Teacher 5	11	9	10	9
Teacher 6	21	2	21	3
Teacher 7	24	0	24	0
Teacher 8	6	18	7	18
Average	13.9	6.75	14.1	6.75

highly consistent. This consistency increases the level of confidence one can have in the rating procedures and the data produced.

Interpretation of the Data Collected

Professor Schulman met with Stayer and Hensen to discuss the results of the evaluation. First, he showed them Table 6.1 (Pretest Data) and explained that the data had been scored reliably. Then he showed them Table 6.2 and indicated that these data also were scored reliably.

He then showed them Tables 6.3 and 6.4. He explained that the effectiveness of the workshop could be evaluated by examining the differences between the pretest and posttest net scores for each teacher. The higher the net score in the positive direction, he explained, the more skillful the teacher was at enhancing the self-esteem of his or her students. A negative net score indicated that a teacher was, on balance, diminishing the self-esteem of his or her students.

Schulman pointed out that the net score of every teacher evaluated improved between the pretest and posttest measures. This was an indication that the workshop had a positive impact. Schulman cautioned, however, that the use of volunteers weakened the case for the effectiveness of the study. He explained that the volunteers might differ from the other participants in the workshop in important ways.

Feedback to Teachers   Sam Schulman scheduled a session with each of the teachers who had participated in the videotaping, and he met with each one privately to view both sets of tapes of their class. While viewing the tapes of the classes, Schulman would stop the tapes in appropriate

TABLE 6.3 Self-Esteem Skills Pretest Net Scores

	Promoting Behaviors (Average of Raters A & B)	Diminishing Behaviors (Average of Raters A & B)	Net Score*
Teacher 1	12.5	8.5	4
Teacher 2	7	8	−1
Teacher 3	2	15	−13
Teacher 4	9.5	7	2.5
Teacher 5	8	11	−3
Teacher 6	14	5.5	8.5
Teacher 7	13	.5	12.5
Teacher 8	2	22	−20
Average	8.5	9.7	−1.2

NOTE: * Net Score = Column 1 minus Column 2.

places to point out an action that either promoted self-esteem or diminished self-esteem. When discussing an action that diminished self-esteem, Schulman would suggest alternate tactics that the teacher could have used. When noting an esteem-building action, Schulman would praise the teacher.

Summary of Evaluation Principles

1. The evaluation was carefully focused using the standards and indicators listed in Resource A of this guide.
2. A behavioral observation scale was carefully designed based both on sound theory and empirical research.
3. The observers used to collect data were carefully trained to collect data accurately and reliably.
4. The integrity and confidentiality of the data were carefully maintained.
5. By meeting with each participant in the study, follow-up and reinforcement of workshop skills were provided.

Alternative Strategies

Other Approaches   The approach used in this evaluation was complex and elaborate. Most school districts will have fewer resources to devote to the evaluation than was the case here. A less elaborate approach could have used a questionnaire administered at the end of the workshop to evaluate the session. Interviews with teachers are another way to collect detailed, complex information about the usefulness of the workshop.

TABLE 6.4 Self-Esteem Skills Posttest Net Scores

	Promoting Behaviors (Average of Raters A & B)	Diminishing Behaviors (Average of Raters A & B)	Net Score*
Teacher 1	18	3.5	14.5
Teacher 2	12	5	7
Teacher 3	3	11	−8
Teacher 4	17	5	12
Teacher 5	10.5	9	1.5
Teacher 6	21	2.5	18.5
Teacher 7	24	0	24
Teacher 8	6.5	18	−11.5
Average	14.0	6.75	7.25

NOTE: * Net Score = Column 1 minus Column 2.

A third approach would have been to measure the self-esteem of the students before and after the training. Such a data collection strategy would have provided a test of the change associated with the workshop. This approach has complex measuring problem, however, because of the age of the children and the very low reliability of changes in scores over so brief a period.

Cautions Regarding Misinterpretation

Videotaping teachers was intrusive. Teachers were aware of the cameras in their classrooms and the reason for the cameras. It is likely that the teachers were particularly careful to use techniques learned in the self-esteem workshop while the cameras were running. There is also no information about how long the changes in teacher behavior lasted. Many newly acquired skills fade with the passage of time unless there is practice and reinforcement.

Resource A: Standards and Indicators of Quality for the Evaluation of Staff Development Programs

Methodology for Selection of Standards and Indicators

Development of the standards and indicators that follow occurred in several stages. An initial set of standards and indicators was developed as part of a research and development project funded by a state department of education. These standards were identified through a comprehensive review of professional literature relevant to the design, implementation, and assessment of staff development programs and a computerized literature search (ERIC).

The comprehensive list of standards and indicators presented in this resource have been refined using the criteria of importance, inclusiveness, potential reliability and validity of measurement, and feasibility of measurement. The standards and indicators presented here are designed to be used by school personnel in planning and conducting internal, developmental evaluations of their staff development programs.

Standards and Indicators of Quality for the Evaluation of Staff Development Programs

Standard 1. **Framework for Staff Development.** Staff development should be conducted within a framework that promotes individual growth and development, provides a positive climate for involvement, and has strong administrative support.

    1.1. The potential benefits of the program should be stressed to participants well before the program begins.

    1.2. Background material that would allow participants to benefit more fully from the program should be provided in advance.

1.3. Participants should be informed of the scheduling of staff development activities well in advance.

1.4. Support for staff development activities should be demonstrated by the principal, other administrators, and professional staff members.

1.5. Opportunities to participate in staff development activities should be presented to staff members in a positive manner.

1.6. Rewards for participation in staff development activities should be provided by the school system.

1.7. Requests to participate in mandatory staff development activities should not be presented in a coercive manner.

1.8. The school should provide compensatory time, pay, or other incentives for participating in staff development activities outside the normal workday.

Standard 2. **Needs Assessment Policy and Procedures.** The school district should have guidelines and procedures for conducting a needs assessment for school-based staff development.

2.1. The needs assessment process should be based on causal analysis.

2.2. The statement of policies and procedures for school-based staff development should be available.

2.3. The school principal and/or the staff development specialist should be able to demonstrate familiarity with and ability to use the needs assessment policies and procedures of the school.

2.4. Records should be available to document the needs assessment conducted for each staff development activity undertaken and completed in the past 3 years.

2.5. Professional Development Plans (PDPs) should be on file for individual staff members.

Standard 3. **Advisory Committee.** The school or school system should have a staff development advisory committee that encourages participation by all parties involved in staff development activities.

3.1. The school should have, or have representation on, a formal committee or other body responsible for the development, conduct, and monitoring of staff development activities.

3.2. The committee should have wide representation from the faculty, staff, and administration of the school.

Standard 4.　**Staff Development Objectives.** The learning objectives and targeted competencies planned for each staff development course and/or activity should be clearly identified and communicated to participants.

4.1.　There should be a syllabus and evaluation standards for each staff development course or activity.

4.2.　There should be written objectives for each staff development course or activity, and the objectives should be linked closely to the needs analysis conducted prior to the development of the program.

4.3.　There should be a written record showing how the program objectives were communicated to participants.

4.4.　There should be a written record of the type of teacher competencies to be developed or enhanced by the staff development activity.

4.5.　The competencies targeted should be related to the deficiencies or other needs identified through the annual evaluation process.

4.6.　The content of the staff development activity should be directly related to the objectives and/or targeted competencies identified.

Standard 5.　**The Instructional Content.** The content of staff development courses and activities should be appropriate to the stated objectives and sufficiently rich and rigorous to achieve those objectives.

5.1.　Staff development materials should be of professional quality and relevant to course or activity objectives.

5.2.　The content of the program should be theoretically sound, up to date, challenging, and efficacious.

5.3.　The school should be able to demonstrate that course content is sufficiently complex to address course or activity objectives.

Standard 6.　**Instructional Process.** The staff development instructional process should be based on adult learning theory and sound instructional practices.

6.1.　The instructional process for staff development courses and activities should be characterized by the presentation of theory, modeling or demonstration, practice, feedback, and coaching.

6.2.　Prior to a staff development course or activity, the school should sponsor readiness activities to prepare participants to get as much benefit from the program as possible.

6.3. The program should be structured to allow participants to benefit from the knowledge and experience of their program cohorts.

6.4. The program should be of sufficient length to have an impact on targeted objectives and competencies.

6.5. Instructional objectives should be consistent with and flow from the overall objectives of the school's or district's staff development program objectives.

6.6. There should be a mechanism for measuring whether or not the staff development courses and objectives have had an impact on targeted objectives and competencies.

6.7. The needs assessment report should link the staff development program to specific job performance expectations or professional development needs of participants.

6.8. Participants' ratings of the staff development program should indicate that the program was perceived as relevant to either their job performance or their professional development needs.

Standard 7.   **Staff Development Trainers.** The staff development trainers should be highly competent and have the backgrounds and experiences necessary to give them high credibility with program participants.

7.1. The trainer should have special expertise in the program content.

7.2. The trainer's background and experience should be similar to the participants', or the trainer should have a well-recognized expertise that lends credibility to his or her efforts.

7.3. The staff development trainer should have the ability to develop rapport with participants and to demonstrate an understanding of the problems, priorities, and needs of participants.

7.4. Trainers should have a demonstrated knowledge of adult learning theory.

7.5. Trainers should be able to incorporate modeling, feedback, and coaching into their instructional strategies.

7.6. Trainers should be able to demonstrate their ability to deliver effective programs.

Standard 8.   **Meeting Course/Activity Objectives.** The school should have a mechanism for determining the extent to which the objectives for staff development courses and activities have been accomplished.

8.1. The school should have written policies and procedures for the evaluation of all staff development courses and activities.

8.2. Follow-up activities should monitor the effectiveness of the application of program content to job activities.

8.3. All staff development programs should be rated for effectiveness by participants.

Standard 9. **Follow-Up and Reinforcement.** The school should follow up staff development programs and activities to ensure that gains made as a result of training are reinforced and maintained.

9.1. There should be systematic procedures for determining the extent to which skills and cognitive materials are applied on the job.

9.2. There should be follow-up activities to reinforce program learning.

Standard 10. **Participant Contribution.** The school should have formal procedures to allow participants to provide input into the evaluation and modification of the school's staff development program.

10.1. Participants in staff development courses and activities should be asked to provide formal input into the assessment and modification of the school's staff development program.

10.2. Participants should have the opportunity to rate the extent to which they perceive that they have input into the development, monitoring, and modification of the staff development program.

Resource B: Bibliography of Selected References

Azzaretto, J. F. (1984). Planning for learning in continuing professional education. *Continuum, 48*(1), 12-18.

Baldwin, T. T., & Fore, J. K. (1988). Transfer of training: A review of the research and directions for future research. *Personnel Psychology, 41,* 63-105.

Brock, W., Dewing, T., Hanson, J. R., Marzano, R. J., Silver, H. F., Strong, R. W., & Wolfe, P. (1990, February). Thoughtful education: Staff development for the 1990s. *Educational Leadership, 47*(5), 25.

Carbo, M., Dunn, R., & Dunn, K. (1989, March). Survey of research on learning styles. *Educational Leadership, 46*(6), 50-58.

Duke, D. L. (1992-1993, December-January). How a staff development plan can rescue at-risk students. *Educational Leadership,* 28-33, 84-85.

Dvorin, R. S. (1986). Evaluation of training. In J. J. Famularo (Ed.), *Handbook of human resource administration* (pp. 26.1-26.12). Oak Park, IL: Moore Publishing.

Edwards, S. (1981). *Changing teacher practice: A synthesis of relevant research.* Austin: Teacher Education University of Texas.

Fielding, G. D. (1985). *Promoting the professional development of teachers and administrators* (Report No. MFO1/PCO4). Eugene, OR: Center for Educational Policy and Management. (ERIC Document Reproduction Service No. ED 260 489)

Ford, J. K. (1984). Introducing new methods for conducting training evaluation and for linking training evaluation to program re-design. *Personnel Psychology, 37*(4), 651-665.

Gall, M. D., & Renchler, T. S. (1985). *Effective staff development for teachers: A research-based model* (Report No. EA 017 615). Eugene: University of Oregon, Clearing House on Educational Management. (ERIC Document Reproduction Service No. ED 265 009)

Geis, G. (1987). Formative evaluation: Developmental testing and expert review. *Performance and Instruction, 26*(4), 1-8.

Georgia Department of Education. (1989, February). *Staff development programs in Georgia under the Quality Basic Education Act,* Atlanta.

Glickman, C. D. (1990, April). Open accountability for the '90s: Between the pillars. *Educational Leadership, 47*(7), 38-42.

Grossnickle, D. R., & Layne, D. J. (1991, September). A shared vision for staff development: Principles, processes, and linkages. *NASSP Bulletin, 75*(536), 88-94.

Guskey, T. R., & Sparks, D. (1991, November). What to consider when evaluating staff development. *Educational Leadership, 49*(3), 73-77.

Hewton, E. (1988). *School focused staff development.* Philadelphia: Falmer Press.

Holly, M. L. (1982). Teachers' views on inservice training. *Phi Delta Kappan, 63,* 417-418.

Howey, J. R. (1985). Six major functions of staff development: An expanded imperative. *Journal of Teacher Education, 36*(1), 58-64.

Iorio, J. E., & Piro, J. M. (1991). Fusing school restructure and staff development: A school district experiment. *Education, 112*(1), 107-119.

Jones, E. V., & Lowe, J. (May 1990). Changing teacher behavior: Effective staff development. *Adult Learning, 1*(7), 8-11.

Kirkpatrick, D. L. (1987). Evaluation. In Robert L. Craig (Ed.), *Training and development handbook: A guide to human resource development* (pp. 301-318). New York: McGraw-Hill.

Kreitlow, B. W. (1990, May). Staff development: What works and why. *Adult Learning, 1*(7), 7.

Lee, L. J., & Sampson, J. F. (1990). A practical approach to program evaluation. *Evaluation and Program Planning, 13*(2), 157-164.

Loucks, S. F., & Melle, M. (1982, April). Evaluation of staff development: How do you know it took? *Journal of Staff Development, 3*(1), 102-117.

Love, A. J. (1983). *Developing effective internal evaluation.* San Francisco: Jossey-Bass.

Macey, W. H. (1982, August). *Linking training needs assessment to training program design.* Paper presented at the 90th Convention of the American Psychological Association, Washington, DC.

Macey, W. H., & Prien, E. P. (1981, August). *Needs assessment: Program and individual development.* Paper presented at the 89th convention of the American Psychological Association, Los Angeles, CA.

Orlich, D. C. (1989, April). Evaluating staff development: Four decision-making models. *Clearing House, 62*(8), 370-374.

Reed, J. (1993). Learner-centered learning. *Training & Development, 47*(6), 20-22.

Russel, J. D., & Blake, B. L. (1988). Formative and summative evaluation of instructional products and learners. *Educational Technology, 28*(7), 22-28.

Rutman, L. (1980). *Planning useful evaluations: Evaluability assessment.* Beverly Hills, CA: Sage.

Schiffer, J. (1980). *School renewal through staff development.* New York: Columbia University, Teachers College Press.

Tibbetts, J. (May 1990). Faces of staff development. *Adult Learning, 1*(7), 6.

Weiss, C. H. (1972). *Evaluation research.* Englewood Cliffs, NJ: Prentice Hall.

Index

In compliance with GPSR, should you have any concerns about the safety of this product, please advise: International Associates Auditing & Certification Limited The Black Church, St Mary's Place, Dublin 7, D07 P4AX Ireland EUAR@ie.ia-net.com